S0-ADA-979

Mughal
Inlay Art

❦ Mughal Inlay Art

R. Nath

Acc No. 5116
Date 6.3.04

Indian History and Culture Society
New Delhi - 110 016

D.K. Printworld (P) Ltd.
New Delhi - 110 015

Cataloging in Publication Data : DK
Nath, R. (Ram), 1933 –
    Mughal inlay art.
    Includes bibliographical references.
    Includes index.

        1. Marquetry — India. 2. Architecture,
    Mogul — India. I. Titile.

ISBN 81-246-0261-1
First Published in India in 2004
© R. Nath

All rights reserved. No part of this publication may be reproduced or transmitted in any form or by any means, electronic or mechanical, including photocopying, recording, or any information storage or retrieval system, without prior written permission.

Published by:
Indian History and Culture Society
B-17 Qutub Institutional Area
New Delhi - 110016

D.K. Printworld (P) Ltd.
Regd. office : 'Sri Kunj', F-52, Bali Nagar
New Delhi - 110 015
Phones : (011) 2545-3975; 2546-6019; Fax : (011) 2546-5926
E-mail: dkprintworld@vsnl.net
Web: www.dkprintworld.com

Printed by : D.K. Printworld (P) Ltd., New Delhi.

Preface

This is study of the *INLAY* art as it developed in Mughal Architecture, from Humayun to Shāh Jehān (*c.* AD 1535-1658) indigenously, and independent of any extraneous inspiration or influence, landmark examples whereof have been cited with illustrations (64 b&w and 16 colour plates). It is wrong to brand it: *pietra-dura* or *pietre-dure* which misnomer was pasted upon it by nineteenth and early twentieth century colonial historians who suffered by a sense of inherent superiority of European culture and art, and who could not believe that the Indian people, whom Macaulay fondly called 'semi-savage,' could develop such a fine and exquisite art as this, which even the classical Greeks and the Romans, who also worked in marbles, could not do!

The claim that Mughal inlay had a Florentine origin was based on the *Orpheus Plaques* which are the solitary example of Florentine *pietra-dura* in Mughal Architecture. As has been discussed in this work, these plaques were imported ready-made and placed in the Throne-Balcony (*Jharokhā*) of the *Dīwān-i-Ām* of Red Fort Delhi, between 1707, after the death of Aurangzeb, and 1824, when Bishop Heber saw them there for the first time, and mentioned them in his travelogue.

Florentine *pietra-dura* had different material, different technique, different motifs and, above all, different background on which it was used. *Pietra-dura* was a picture-art used on wooden

5

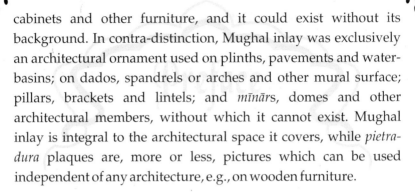

cabinets and other furniture, and it could exist without its background. In contra-distinction, Mughal inlay was exclusively an architectural ornament used on plinths, pavements and water-basins; on dados, spandrels or arches and other mural surface; pillars, brackets and lintels; and *mīnār*s, domes and other architectural members, without which it cannot exist. Mughal inlay is integral to the architectural space it covers, while *pietra-dura* plaques are, more or less, pictures which can be used independent of any architecture, e.g., on wooden furniture.

INLAY (*pachchīkārī* or *parchīnkārī*) is the distinctive ornamentation of Mughal Architecture as Glazed-tiling (*kāshīkārī*) was of Iranian Architecture and Glass-mosaic (*shīshākārī*) was of Byzantine Architecture. It is also the most distinctive characteristic of the Shahjehanian phase of Mughal Architecture which marks the zenith of this style. A historical appraisal of the evolutionary process of its growth and development, to the elegance of the Taj dados, aptly called the *chef d'oeu-vre* of Indian art, is absolutely needed for a thorough understanding and appreciation of its originality and creativeness, over and above the misnomers imposed upon it by European authors.

My thanks are due to my friend Dr. S.P. Gupta for his interest in this work; and to Shri Susheel Kumar Mittal of D.K. Printworld for its nice design commensurate with the subject.

Agra: 5 December 2003   **R. Nath**

Contents

Preface   5
Abbreviations   8
List of Illustrations   9

1. The "Orpheus Plaques" and the Florentine   13
   "Pietra-dura" Controversy
   - (a) The Orpheus Plaques of Red Fort Delhi   13
   - (b) Their Material, Ground and Motifs   17
   - (c) Technique of Inlay and Mosaic   19
   - (d) 'Orpheus Plaques' were imported Ready-made   20

2. Evolution on Inlay Art in Mughal Architecture   32

Appendix
Mughal Forms: Exotic or Indigenous   109

Index   115

Abbreviations

ASI AR	:	Archaeological Survey of India, *Annual Report*
Bernier	:	*Travels in Moghal Empire* by Francois Bernier; ed. A Constable (Delhi rep. 1972)
BNL	:	*Bādshāh-Nāmah* of 'Abdul Ḥamīd Lāhaurī, Bibliotheca Indica Series of the Asiatic Society of Bengal, Calcutta, 2 vols. (Calcutta 1866-68)
CDMA	:	R. Nath, *Colour Decoration in Mughal Architecture* (2nd ed., Jaipur 1990)
Dixon-IJ-II	:	J.S. Dixon, 'Florentine Mosaic: Mughal Inlay' in *Indologica-Jaipurensia,* II (1996) Agra, pp. 54-73
Fergusson	:	James Fergusson, *History of Indian & Eastern Architecture,* revised & ed. by J. Burgess, 2 vols. (Delhi, rep. 1967)
HMA	:	R. Nath, *History of Mughal Architecture,* Vol. I (New Delhi, 1982); Vol. II (New Delhi, 1985); Vol. III (New Delhi, 1994); Vol. IV Part-1 (to be released)
Koch	:	Ebba Koch, *Shah Jahan and Orpheus* (Graz, 1988)
Windsor	:	*King of the World : The Badshah-Namah* (An Imperial Mughal Manuscript from the Royal Library Windsor Castle); ed. by M.C. Beach and Ebba Koch (London, 1997)

List of Illustrations

Pl. 1. **Throne Balcony** (*Jharokhā*), *Dīwān-i-'Ām* (1639-48), Red Fort Delhi

Pl. 2. *Banglā* (Pavilion) of the Throne Balcony, *Dīwān-i-'Ām*, Red Fort Delhi

Pl. 3. *Orpheus Plaques, Dīwān-i-'Ām*

Pl. 4. Throne Balcony, *Dīwān-i-'Ām* (1628-35), Agra Fort

Pl. 5. Inlaid Designs on the Central Arch, *Qal'ā-i-Kuhnā Masjid* (1533-40), Old Fort Delhi

Pl. 6. Inlaid Designs on the Central Arch, *Qal'ā-i-Kuhnā Masjid* (1533-40), Old Fort Delhi

Pl. 7. Inlaid Designs, *Sher-Mandal* (1533-40), Old Fort Delhi

Pl. 8. Inlaid Designs on the Intrados, Central Arch, *Qal'ā-i-Kuhnā Masjid*

Pl. 9. Inlaid Designs, *Tomb of Atagah Khān* (1566-67), Delhi

Pl. 10. *Tomb of Humāyūn* (*c.* 1558-70), Delhi

Pl. 11. Inlaid Stone Work, *Tomb of Humāyūn*

Pl. 12. *Hāthī-Pol*, Delhi Gate (1568-69) Agra Fort, with Inlaid Motifs

Pl. 13. Inlaid *Gaja-Vyāla*s (Composite animal with elephant-head), *Hāthī-Pol,* Agra Fort

Pl. 14. Inlaid Ducks, *Hāthī-Pol*, Agra Fort

Pl. 15. Western Façade of the (so-called) *Jehāngīrī- Mahal* (1569), Agra Fort

Pl. 16. Inlaid Designs on the Portal, *Jehāngīrī-Mahal*, Agra Fort

Pl. 17. White Marble Framing of Red Stone Arches, Western Façade of the *Jehāngīrī-Mahal* (1565-69), Agra Fort

Pl. 18. White Marble Framing of Red Stone Arches, Eastern Façade of the *Jehāngīrī-Mahal* (1565-69), Agra Fort

Pl. 19. Inlaid Designs, *Bādshāhī- Darwāzah, Jāmi' Masjid* (1564-72), Fatehpur Sikri

Pl. 20. Inlay Work on the *Buland-Darwāzah* (1601), *Jāmi' Masjid*, Fatehpur Sikri

Pl. 21. Inlaid Designs, *Jāmi' Masjid* (1564-72), Fatehpur Sikri

Pl. 22. Inlaid Designs on the *Mihrābs, Jāmi' Masjid* (1564-72), Fatehpur Sikri

Pl. 23. Inlaid Designs on the *Mihrābs, Jāmi' Masjid* (1564-72), Fatehpur Sikri

Pl. 24. Inlay and Mosaic on the Main (South) Gate, *Akbar's Tomb* (1605-12),

Sikandara Agra

Pl. 25. Inlay and Mosaic on the Main (South) Gate, *Akbar's Tomb* (1605-12), Sikandara Agra

Pl. 26. Inlaid Designs on the Mural Surface, Main (South) Gate, *Akbar's Tomb* (1605-12), Agra

Pl. 27. Inlaid Designs on the Mural Surface, Main Gate, *Akbar's Tomb* (1605-12), Agra

Pl. 28. Inlaid Designs on the Mural Surface, Main Gate, *Akbar's Tomb* (1605-12), Agra

Pl. 29. Inlaid Designs on the Mural Surface, Main Gate, *Akbar's Tomb* (1605-12), Agra

Pl. 30. Inlaid Designs on the Mural Surface, Main Gate, *Akbar's Tomb* (1605-12), Agra

Pl. 31. Inlaid Stylized Arabesques on the Spandrels of Arch, Main Gate, *Akbar's Tomb* (1605-12), Agra

Pl. 32. Inlaid Stylized Arabesques on the Spandrels of Arch, Main Gate, *Akbar's Tomb* (1605-12), Agra

Pl. 33. Inlaid Panels on the *Īwān*-Portal, Main Tomb, *Akbar's Tomb* (1605-12), Agra

Pl. 34. Inlay on the *Īwān*, Eastern Gate, *Akbar's Tomb* (1605-12), Agra

Pl. 35. Inlaid Designs, revealing sockets, Eastern Gate, *Akbar's Tomb,* Agra

Pl. 36. Inlaid Arabesques on the top and spandrels of the *Īwan*, Western Gate, *Akbar's Tomb,* Agra

Pl. 37. Inlaid Designs, Western Gate, *Akbar's Tomb* (1605-12), Agra

Pl. 38. Inlaid White Marble on Red Stone Relief, Eastern Gate, *Akbar's Tomb* (1605-12), Agra

Pl. 39. Inlaid White Marble on Red Stone Relief, Eastern Gate, *Akbar's Tomb* (1605-12), Agra

Pl. 40. White Marble Dado, with Inlaid Border, Second Storey Hall, Western Gate, *Akbar's Tomb,* Agra

Pl. 41. Inlay Work on the Eastern (Main) Gate, *Tomb of I'timād-ud-Daulah* (1622-28), Agra

Pl. 42. Tomb of *I'timād-ud-Daulah* (1622-28), Agra

Pl. 43. Inlay Work on the Exterior Mural Surface, *Tomb of I'timād-ud-Daulah* (1622-28), Agra

Pl. 44. Inlaid Designs (*guldastās,* vases, cups and dishes), *Tomb of I'timād-ud-Daulah* (1622-28), Agra

Pl. 45. Inlaid Designs (cypress, fruits, cup and dish), *Tomb of I'timād-ud-Daulah* (1622-28), Agra

Pl. 46. Inlaid Arabesques on the Spandrels of Arch, *Tomb of I'timād-ud-Daulah* (1622-28), Agra

Pl. 47. Inlaid Designs on Towers, *Tomb of I'timād-ud-Daulah* (1622-28), Agra

Pl. 48. Inlaid Designs on Towers, *Tomb of I'timād-ud-Daulah* (1622-28), Agra

Pl. 49. Inlaid Stylized Arabesque on the Pavement of the Upper Pavilion, *Tomb of I'timād-ud-Daulah* (1622-28), Agra

Pl. 50. Inlay Art on the Dados, Spandrels and other Mural Surface, *Muthamman Burj (Shāh Burj)* (1631-40), Agra Fort

Pl. 51. Inlaid Water-Basin, sunk in the Pavement, *Muthamman Burj (Shāh Burj)* (1631-40), Agra Fort

Pl. 52. Dado with Inlaid Border, *Muthamman Burj (Shāh Burj)* (1631-40), Agra Fort

Pl. 53. Dado with Inlaid Border, *Dīwān-ī-Khāṣ* (1635), Agra Fort

Pl. 54. Inlaid Designs with *Ghaṭa-Pallava*, Bases of Pillars, *Dīwān-ī-Khāṣ* (1635), Agra Fort

Pl. 55. Inlaid Water-Basin, *Rang Mahal* (1639-48), Red Fort Delhi

Pl. 56. Portal Dado with Inlaid Border, *Tāj Mahal* (1631-48), Agra

Pl. 57. Dados of the Main Cenotaph-Hall, with *Ghaṭa-Pallava* and Inlaid Border, *Tāj Mahal* (1631-48), Agra

Pl. 58. *Jālī* Screen (*Jhajjharī*) with Inlaid Borders and Cresting, *Tāj Mahal* (1631-48), Agra

Pl. 59. Marble Cenotaphs with Inlaid Designs, *Tāj Mahal* (1631-48), Agra

Pl. 60. Inlaid Quranic Verses, Cenotaph Hall, *Tāj Mahal* (1631-48), Agra

Pl. 61. Inlaid Designs on Spandrels of Arches, Turrets, Pinnacles and Friezes, *Tāj Mahal* (1631-48), Agra

Pl. 62. Inlaid Arabesques on the Spandrels of the Arch, *Tāj Mahal* (1631-48), Agra

Pl. 63. Inlay Work on the *Mīnār, Tāj Mahal* (1631-48), Agra

Pl. 64. Inlay Art on the *Tāj Mahal* (1631-48) Agra, in beautiful tints and tones

Colour Plates

Col. Pl. I. Back Wall of the Throne-Balcony (*Jharokhā*), *Dīwān-i-'Ām*, Red Fort, Delhi (photo courtesy: Ebba Koch's *Shah Jahan and Orpheus*)

Col. Pl. II. Central Plaque depicting Orpheus playing to animals, Throne-Balcony (*Jharokhā*), *Dīwān-i-'Ām*, Red Fort Delhi (photo courtesy: Ebba Koch's *Shah Jahan and Orpheus*)

Col. Pl. III. Plaque with bird, set on the side of a wooden cabinet, Italy, 17th century (photo courtesy: Ebba Koch's *Shah Jahan and Orpheus*)

Col. Pl. IV. Vase with flowers, set on the central door of a wooden cabinet, Italy, 17th century (photo courtesy: Ebba Koch's *Shah Jahan and Orpheus*)

Col. Pl. V. Wooden Cabinet with birds, flowers and flower vases in *pietra-dure*,

Italy, 17th century (photo courtesy: Ebba Koch's *Shah Jahan and Orpheus*)

Col. Pl. VI. Wooden Cabinet with a large plaque of Orpheus on the central door and small plaques with animals on the front of the drawers in *pietra-dura*, Italy, *c.* middle of the 17th century, Chirk Castle, Cloyd, Greet Britain (photo courtesy: Ebba Koch's *Shah Jahan and Orpheus*)

Col. Pl. VII. Inlay Art on the Throne Pavilion, *Dīwān-i-'Ām* (1628-35), Agra Fort

Col. Pl. VIII. Inlaid Designs on the Entrance Portal of the so-called *Jehāngīrī-Mahal* (1565-69), Agra Fort

Col. Pl. IX. Inlaid Designs on the *Qiblah* Wall of the *Jāmi' Masjid* (1564-72), Fatehpur Sikri

Col. Pl. X. Inlaid Designs on the Main (South) Gateway of Akbar's Tomb (1605-12), Sikandara Agra

Col. Pl. XI. Inlaid Designs on the *Īwān*-Portal of the Main Building, Akbar's Tomb (1605-12) Agra

Col. Pl. XII. Inlaid Designs on the Exterior of the Western Gate, Akbar's Tomb (1605-12), Agra

Col. Pl. XIII. Inlaid Designs on the Exterior of the Tomb of I'timād-ud Daulah (1622-28), Agra

Col. Pl. XIV. Inlaid Designs, *Muthamman Burj (Shāh-Burj)* (1631-40), Agra Fort

Col. Pl. XV. Inlaid Dados, Tāj Maḥal (1631-48), Agra

Col. Pl. XVI. Inlaid Spandrels of Arch, Tāj Maḥal (1631-48), Agra

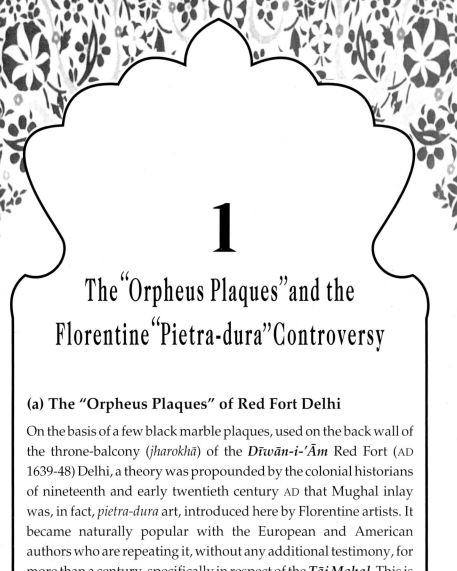

1

The "Orpheus Plaques" and the Florentine "Pietra-dura" Controversy

(a) The "Orpheus Plaques" of Red Fort Delhi

On the basis of a few black marble plaques, used on the back wall of the throne-balcony (*jharokhā*) of the *Dīwān-i-'Ām* Red Fort (AD 1639-48) Delhi, a theory was propounded by the colonial historians of nineteenth and early twentieth century AD that Mughal inlay was, in fact, *pietra-dura* art, introduced here by Florentine artists. It became naturally popular with the European and American authors who are repeating it, without any additional testimony, for more than a century, specifically in respect of the *Tāj Maḥal*. This is an important matter and it must be examined in necessary details.[1]

The wall of the *Dīwān-i-'Ām*,[2] overlooking the central bay, has a white marble throne-balcony, called *jharokhā* (Pl. 1), protected by a jalied balustrade. On its two sides are seats with pedestals, just for giving an exquisite architectural effect to the balcony. In its front, attached to it, is a beautiful *'bunglah'* (*banglā*) pavilion, also of white marble, having four tapering

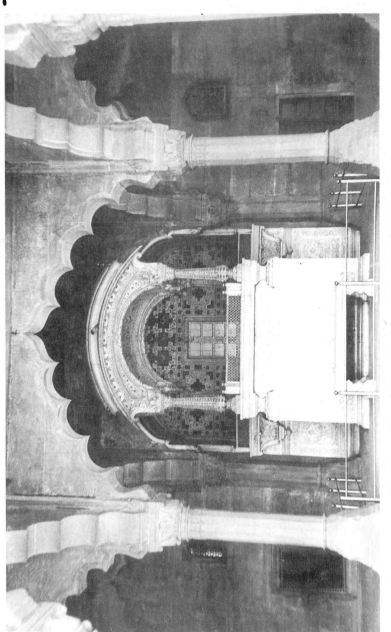

Pl. 1 ***Throne Balcony*** *(Jharokha), Diwan-i-'Am (1639–48),* Red Fort Delhi

Pl. 2 *Bangla* (Pavilion) of the Throne Balcony, *Diwan-i-'Am* Red Fort Delhi

Pl. 3 *Orpheus Plaques, Diwan-i-'Am*

pillars,[3] supporting semi-circular arches,[4] on the four sides, and a curved, *ladāo*, technically *bānglādār* ceiling. The *chhajjā* which protects the arches externally is also correspondingly circular, with sharp overhanging edges at the corners, where it is supported on brackets (*Pl.* 2). The whole of it is built of pure white marble and is gorgeously **inlaid** by polychrome, semi-precious stones in a wide variety of stylized floral designs. All this belongs to the architectural style of Shāh Jehān, in letter and in spirit.

But the back wall of this throne-balcony has been differently treated. Square and oblong plaques of **black marble** have been embedded in the white marble mural surface, in a bizarre order. These plaques have **inlaid designs composed of birds** perched among twigs, leaves and flowers (*Col. Pl.* I) Floral designs, both realistic and stylized, some with birds, have also been depicted, in inlay, in interspaces between the plaques, on the white marble surface which forms their background. Above all these panels is the one, with a semi-circular top, depicting *Orpheus* playing guitar or violin to animals (*Pl.* 3 and *Col. Pl.* II). It is said to be a copy of the famous sixteenth-century painting by Raphael. Altogether, there are some 270 black marble plaques.[5] These are called '*Orpheus Plaques.*'

(b) Their Material, Ground and Motifs

It is important to note that the "inlay" work on the *Orpheus Plaques* is completely different from that on the *bunglah* and the throne-balcony, and even that on the white marble background on which these plaques are embedded. These plaques are made **of different material**: a deep black marble which was not found in India, and which was available only in Italy. This art, called *pietra-dura* is also **different in technique** from the Mughal inlay art (*pachchīkārī* or *parchīnkārī*) which developed in India indigenously from Humāyūn to Shāh Jehān (*c.* 1535 to 1658), as shall be studied hereinafter, inasmuch as it (i.e., *pietra-dura*) was a section mosaic (*opus sectile*), made in **panels or plaques with defined borders, on a stone or wooden background, which it dominated like a picture (as on back walls and wooden cabinets)**, while the Mughal inlay was primarily **architectural.** *Pietra-Dura* panels were used as pictures, or wall-hangings or *pichhwāīs*, rather than on architectural parts, e.g., pavements, pillars, brackets, lintels, dados and spandrels of arches, for architectural ornamentation to accelerate the architectural nuances. The *'pietra-dura'* was essentially a **picture-art** and these plaques were also designed as pictures with defined borders and they **have no architectural context or relevance.**

Precisely *'pietra-dura'* was a **picture-art,** while **Mughal inlay was architectural.**

Their **motifs are also different.** No birds have been shown anywhere else on any white marble building of Shāh Jehān and **'Orpheus plaques'** are the only example of their use in Mughal architecture. Such birds were depicted in Mughal miniature paintings, particularly on the borders (*hāshiyahs*), and also on carpets, curtains and *chandovās*,[6] but there is no instance of their use in Mughal architecture. In fact, these plaques had no impact on the development of Mughal art of inlay or the style, and these were never a part of its evolutionary process. **These were used here only as CURIOS, only ONCE.**

The way this panelling has been done with black marble square and oblong plaques on a white marble background is also unusual and unprecedented. There is no other example in Mughal Architecture. It creates a monotony and it is **un-Mughal.** The Mughal artist avoided **architectural monotony** the most, and he had several ingenious ways to dispense with it. There are too many straight lines and **these panels are anachronistic** in the age of Shāh Jehān when overall emphasis was laid on deep and sharp **curved lines,** rather than on such misjoined straight ones, which fact the adjoining *bunglah* just testifies.

Orpheus plaques are the only specimen of this art in Mughal Architecture. This is essentially a Florentine work, executed by a Florentine artist and, in all probability, these plaques were imported readymade and placed at such a respectable position. It could not have been made here, *in-situ*, by Jeronimo Veroneo, the Venetian, who was a goldsmith and jeweller and died at Lahore in 1640; nor by Austin or Augustine of Bordeaux, the Frenchman, who was a jeweller and expert in counterfeiting precious stone, as his own letters testify,[7] and who died at Chaul in 1632; or by any other European artist, as the foundations of the new city of Shāh Jehān at Delhi, viz., Shāhjehānābād and its citadel, the Red Fort, were laid in 1639, and the throne-balcony of the *Dīwān-i-'Ām* is a later work.

(c) Technique of Inlay and Mosaic

It must be explained that in INLAY, whether executed on a red sandstone or white marble slab, grooves (or sockets) were made in accordance with the design, and were filled in by stone pieces of different colours, making up that design. Because stones were "**laid in**" it was called **INLAY** and, technically, it was **Inlaid Mosaic**. In this case, the **stone slab provides a background** to the design.

On the other hand, it is only MOSAIC if the design is wholly made up of pieces of stones placed on a slab or plaster, i.e., when the design paves or covers the whole surface. It is **OVERLAY** (laid over) and, technically, it is "Tessellated Mosaic" or, simply, "**Mosaic**." The stone slab or plaster does not provide a background to the design which stands independent of it.

The Mughal inlay which developed from Humāyūn's *Dīn-Panāh* (Old Fort) Delhi (*c.* 1535) independently, the various stages of whose evolutionary process down to the *Tāj Maḥal* (1631-48) can be systematically traced, as studied hereinafter, belongs to the former class. Florentine inlay, called *'pietra-dura,'* to denote the form of inlay of shaped pieces of coloured stones in grooves cut in marble, i.e., **intarsia,** also belongs, technically, to this class. It is also section-mosaic (*opus sectile*), either in *pietre-dure* (hard stones) or *pietre-tenere* (soft stones).

But there are fundamental differences in the two arts.

Besides the **difference of material** — that Mughal inlay was executed in sandstone slabs, forming the background, from Humāyūn (1530-40; 1555) to Akbar (1556-1605), and for some time also under Jehāngīr (1605-27), and in white marble slabs thereafter, and exclusively under Shāh Jehān (1628-58), while Florentine mosaic was executed in black marble available only in Italy, there is also a subtle **difference of technique.** Florentine *pietra-dura* was section mosaic executed **on a stone or wooden background which it dominated like a picture. Hence it was largely used on back-walls or wooden cabinets** (*Col. Pl.* III to VI). The Mughal inlay was used, on the other hand, on pavements, dados, pillars, brackets, lintels, spandrels of arches and, of course, on other parts of Mughal buildings, to enhance the background into which patterns of coloured stones were inlaid. Hence, **it was an architectural ornament** and its form, in either case, was determined by the background on which it was executed. Thus, an inlaid design used on an arch-spandrel cannot be applied on a dado or a pillar and, in fact, it cannot stand without it. **It is integral to the architectural space it covers.** The Florentine *pietra-dura* specimens are more or less pictures and can be used independent of any architecture, e.g., on **wooden furniture**, on which this art has been, in fact, more popularly displayed.[8]

(d) Orpheus Plaques were Imported Ready-made

Dixon's is the latest study on this subject and this is how he has analysed the phenomenon of the appearance of *Orpheus plaques* in India :

Actually the wall (the back wall of the throne balcony of *Diwan-i-'Am* Red Fort with the *'Orpheus plaques'* is something of an oddity. On each side of the door in the centre of the wall are two rectangular spaces the height of the door, each space being bordered by a series of small square panels of Florentine mosaic depicting flowers, fruits and birds on a black marble background, the panels themselves being let into the white marble setting of the wall. Within these four spaces are other similar panels arranged symmetrically round larger panels of birds and vases of flowers. Above the height of the door and extending the whole width of the wall is another space with a series of symmetrical group of large and small panels, the whole with a border of the small panels. There are about 24 large and medium-sized panels and at least 240 of the small panels, all of which are of the type of **Florentine mosaic set in a background of black marble of which many examples, displayed inset in furniture** (*Col. Pl.* III to VI), **mainly cabinets, have been preserved.**[9] There can be no doubt that all these panels follow Italian designs and scarcely less doubt that **Marshall was right in thinking that the panels were an Italian import into India.**[10]

Lando Bartoli, a former Director of the *opificio delle Pietre Dure*, affirmed in a paper read in 1983 that the panels are faithful in design to those produced in Florence **for the embellishment of Cabinets and other pieces of furniture.**[11]

For a better understanding of the *Orpheus plaques* and chronology of their appearance in the *Dīwān-i-'Ām* Red Fort Delhi, reference must be made to the throne balcony *jharokha* of the *Dīwān-i-'Ām* of Agra Fort (1628-35).[12] It is a three-arched, profusely inlaid white marble, oblong chamber (*Pl.* 4). **Cusped**

Pl. 4 Throne Balcony, *Diwan-i-'Am* (1628-35), Agra Fort

niches have been sunk into the walls of the interior. Every mural surface — even the ceiling — has been inlaid in polychrome, with stylized floral designs (*Col. Pl.* VII) which are characteristic of the art of Shāh Jehān's age. Anything similar to the *Orpheus plaques* is not there. Lahauri, the contemporary historian of Shāh Jehān, described it, in 1636-37, and noted that this *jharokha* was not previously so elaborately ornamented but now, in this august reign, it was built of white marble and its walls were inlaid with precious stones of various colours (*ān aḥjār shamīnah rangārang parchīn kardah*).[13] He also referred to the niches of the *jharokhā* as *Chīnī-khānah* wherein vessels inlaid with precious stones were laid. There is no mention at all of any panels similar to the *Orpheus plaques* of the *Dīwān-i-'Ām* Red Fort Delhi.

Nor does he, or any other contemporary or later Persian historian, or foreign traveller, make even the slightest allusion to the *Orpheus plaques* in the *Dīwān-i-'Ām* Red Fort Delhi, and these plaques have not been mentioned, at all, during the period from 1638 to 1658 (Shāh Jehān) or from 1658 to 1707 (Aurangzeb). Such a keen observer as Francis Bernier visited the Mughal court (1659-65) and he has left seventeenth-century description of Agra and Delhi, and their Royal buildings. He noticed the *Dīwān-i-'Ām* and the throne-balcony:

> . . . a large and magnificent hall, decorated with several rows of pillars, which, as well as the ceiling, are all painted and overlaid with gold. . . . In the centre of the wall that separates the hall from the Seraglio, and higher from the floor than a man can reach, is **a wide and lofty opening, or large window** (throne-balcony) where the Monarch every day, about noon, sits upon his throne. . . . Immediately under the throne is an enclosure, surrounded by silver rails. . . .[14]

He did not find the *Orpheus plaques* on its back wall, otherwise he would have been too glad to mention these curios in his travelogue, for the proud enlightenment of his countrymen. This shows that these panels were not there during the reign of Shāh Jehān.

It must be noted that glass from Aleppo was imported and used in the *Shīsh-Maḥal* of Agra Fort in Shāh Jehān's age and this fact has been faithfully recorded in the Persian histories of his reign and this material is named *Shishaye-Halebī* (the Aleppo Glass).[15] But the import of these *pietra-dura* plaques has not been recorded in these histories which shows that they did not come during his age.

It appears that Bishop Heber was the first traveller who noticed the *Orpheus plaques* in the *Dīwān-i-'Ām* Red Fort Delhi, in 1824. He mentioned :

> Mosaic paintings (?) of birds, animals and flowers, and in the centre, what decides the point of their being the work of Italian, or at least European artists, a small group of **Orpheus playing to the beasts.**[16]

James Fergusson was the first art-historian who studied these buildings authoritatively during the period from 1835 to 1845. He noticed the throne-balcony and its inlay work as follows :

> .... the *Diwan-i-'Am* or great audience hall of the palace, very similar in design to that of Agra but more magnificent . . . in its centre is a highly ornamental niche, in which on a platform of marble richly inlaid with precious stones....[17]

In the accompanying footnote, he continued :

> When we took possession of the palace, every one seems to have **looted** after the most independent fashion. Among others, a Captain (afterwards Sir John) Jones tore up a great part of this platform, but had the happy idea to

get his **loot** set in marble as table tops. Two of these he brought home and sold to the Government for £ 500, and placed in the Indian Museum. **No one can doubt that the one with the birds was executed by Florentine, or at least Italian artists;** while the other already mentioned, which was apparently at the back of the platform is a bad copy from Raphael's picture of Orpheus charming the beasts. As is well known, that was again a copy of a picture in the catacombs. There Orpheus is playing on a lyre, in Raphael's picture on a violin, and that is the instrument represented in the Delhi mosaic. Even if other evidence were wanting, this would be sufficient to set the question at rest. It certainly was not put there by the bigot Aurangzeb.[18]

When did Captain Jones tore up the throne-balcony — in 1803, just after the capture of the Red Fort by the British, or some time during the rule of the East India Company (1803-57), has yet to be investigated.[19] But, it is true that had this **human figure and birds** been there, just on the back wall of the throne-balcony where he held his *durbār*, Aurangzeb could not have tolerated them and he would have destroyed them the way he destroyed the elephant-sculptures of the Delhi-Gate of this Fort.

This shows that **these plaques were not executed here** *in-situ*, **but were imported readymade**[20] and placed there either some time during the eighteenth-century, or the early rule of the East India Company. Most probably, there originally were some panels bearing encaustic golden paintings, or paintings with *mīnākārī* and precious stones, or some such other extremely valuable set of panels. Contemporary historian Kambo's statement that this "is famed for its various coloured stones inlaid into the wall and which, through the skill of excellent art workers, has been adorned with many **rare pictures** (*taṣwīr*) and a railing of pure gold on three sides"[21] confirms this. It appear that, in the background of inlaid (stylized floral) designs (which were typically Mughal and which have partially survived), **figurative paintings** depicting scenes from Mughal life, and finished with gold and precious stones, were originally set on this wall. These were all plundered in the later ages (like similar paintings of the *Khās-Maḥal* Agra Fort) and, subsequently, **the wall was redone** with these imported *Orpheus plaques* leaving portions of the original inlay work of the background. Had these plaques been there when Kambo made his record, he would have certainly mentioned them and figures of Orpheus, birds and beasts, and he would have described them as "imported" or "copied" from some foreign work. That he did not do this well explains that these plaques were not there in Shāh Jehān's age.

The conscientious art-historian Havell also had a similar view:

In my opinion, the Delhi *pietra-dura* has been wrongly attributed to Shāh Jehān's reign. It has all the appearance of **eighteenth-century work** and, as far as I am aware, there is no evidence worth considering to show that it existed previous to the reign to Aurangzeb.[22]

John Marshall, the Director-General of the A.S.I., under whose supervision the *Orpheus plaques* were restored (1902-9), studied them closely and analysis of this eminent archaeologist has thrown a flood of light on this subject. Thus he noted :

. . . . mosaic work of marble and coloured stones with which its entire surface was adorned. The decoration is more particularly famous for the panels of black marble, inlaid with a variety of coloured stones in designs of birds and flowers. **These panels are the sole examples in India of this particular form of technique.** The most justly famous among them is one representing the **figure of Orpheus** sitting under a tree, and fiddling to a circle of listening animals. (These were plundered in 1857 and 12 panels were sold by Captain (Sir John) Jones for £ 500 to the British Government who deposited them in the South Kensington Museum. (These were restored with great care by Major H. H. Cole, Curator of Ancient Monuments in India in 1882), but unhappily some of the stones employed in the new work matched badly with the originals. The difference between them is particularly noticeable in the background of the panels; a greyish black Indian marble having been used to replace the intensely black and fine-grained marble, only procurable in Italy. In some other respects also the new work is inferior, the designs being harsher and the technique coarser. (Some panels could not be restored. . .) and it will very probably be found necessary to get the panels executed in Florence or to obtain artists from Italy to do the work in India ... the black marble of their backgrounds and the majority of **inlaid stones are of Italian, and not Indian, provenance,** and it is not unreasonable to suppose, therefore, that **they were not only designed but actually executed in an Italian studio and afterwards imported into the country.** The arabesques, on the other hand, which decorate the interspaces between the panels are of pure Indian style and Indian workmanship without a vestige of foreign influence.[23]

Marshall reiterated this in a subsequent writing when he discussed the indigenous development of Mughal inlay :

The designs executed in it are essentially **oriental** in character;[24] and even as regards technique, it is more probable that it originated independently in this country. This view is not a new one, but it has lately received strong confirmation from the discovery at the Khalji mausoleum at Mandu of *pietra-dura* work in rougher and earlier stage than was hitherto known. Nor can the plaques in the Delhi throne referred to above (i.e., the *Orpheus plaques*) be taken as evidence in this matter. For, as I have demonstrated elsewhere,[25] **these panels were, without doubt, made in Italy itself and brought to India all complete;** so that they stand on quite a different plane to works of art produced on Indian soil and afford no substantial proof whatever of the extraneous influences to be looked for in the latter.[26]

He observed in a footnote, in continuation:

The view which I then expressed has since been confirmed by S. Menegatti, a Florentine mosaicista and a practical expert in Italian marbles.[27] . . . . The presence of these Italian plaques demonstrates trade connections but nothing more.[28]

This discussion confirms, unequivocally, that the *Orpheus plaques* were not made in India and **were imported readymade** from Italy (Florence) and placed there, some time after Aurangzeb.

References

1. This subject has been widely debated and scholars are writing on it even in recent times, e.g., Ebba Koch, *Shah Jahan and Orpheus* (Graz 1988) (hereinafter abb. *Koch*) and J.S. Dixon, "Florentine Mosaic: Mughal Inlay" in *Indologica Jaipurensia* Agra, vol. II (1996) 54-73 (hereinafter abb. *Dixon-IJ*-II). Also see this author's *Colour Decoration in Mughal Architecture* (2nd ed. Jaipur, 1990) (hereinafter abb. *CDMA*) 65-68.

2. This building has been studied in full details in this author's *History of Mughal Architecture* (abb. *HMA*), vol. IV, Part 1, Chapter 3, under the sub-head : *The Diwan-i-'Am of Red fort Delhi* (1639-48).

3. These are erroneously called '*baluster columns*' by *Koch, op. cit.*

4. These are not full semi-circular but segmental circular.

5. *Dixon-IJ*-II, 54-73.

6. As for example, in the *King of the World : The Badshah-Namah* (An Imperial Mughal Manuscript from the Royal Library Windsor Castle) (ed. by M.C.

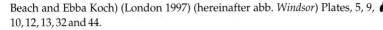

Beach and Ebba Koch) (London 1997) (hereinafter abb. *Windsor*) Plates, 5, 9, 10, 12, 13, 32 and 44.

7. For details, see R. Nath, "Augustine of Bordeaux and His Relations with the Mughal Court (1612-32)," *Quarterly Review of Historical Studies*, Calcutta, VIII. 3 (1968-69) 157-64. His four letters were published in the *Journal of the Punjab Historical Society*, vol. IV, no. 1 (Calcutta 1916).

8. For example, see *Koch* Pls. 22 to 26, 27 and 40; and the following references made by Dixon. He noted categorically that Florentine mosaic was largely produced for **purposes** different from those of Mughal inlay and it cannot match the **scale** or the delicacy of the designs used at the Taj or in the palaces of Agra and Delhi fort, cf. *Dixon-IJ*-II, 63.

9. Dixon's footnote reads as follows : "Examples of these panels or plaques included those inset in a **cabinet** (W. 24-1977) in the Victoria and Albert Museum, London, as well as similar plaques decorating **cabinets** on display in the museums at Florence. **Many other examples of similarly decorated FURNITURE** are held in privately or publicly owned buildings in Italy, Britain, France and Germany. See also the illustration of a cabinet, *circa* 1615, in Jones, W. E., "Antiques : Pictured in Stone" in *Architectural Digest* (U. S. A.), November 1982, p. 123" cf. *Dixon-IJ*-II, p. 72

10. *Ibid.*, p. 66.

11. *Ibid.*, 66-67 and ref. 49.

12. It has been studied in full details in *HMA*-IV, Part 1, Chapter 3, under the sub-head : "(1) *The Diwan-i-'Am of Agra Fort* (1628-35)."

13. *Badshah Namah* of 'Abdul Hamid Lahauri, Persian Text, *Bibliotheca Indica* series of the Asiatic Society of Bengal Calcutta, vol. I (Part I-II), Calcutta (1866) vol. II (Calcutta 1868), (hereinafter abb. *BNL*), I. II. 236.

14. *Travels in the Moghal Empire* by Francois Bernier (ed. A. Constable) (Delhi rep. 1972) (hereinafter abb. *Bernier*) 260-61.

15. For full details, see *HMA*-IV, Part 1, Chapter 4, sub-head : "(a) (3) *The Shish-Mahal* (1631-40)."

16. Bishop Reginald Heber, *Narrative of Journey through the Upper Provinces of India*, 2 vols (London 1828), vol. I, p. 562.

17. James *Fergusson, History of Indian and Eastern Architecture* (revised & ed. by J. Burgess) 2 vols. (hereinafter abb. *Fergusson*) (Delhi 1967), II. 311.

18. *Ibid.*, 311, ftn. 1. We presume that this is Fergusson's own note and not of his editor James Burgess. Dixon has written at length on the identity of this Orpheus and it would be enlightening to quote him : "while the wall might be an oddity in Mughal architecture, the **Orpheus panel is decidedly incongruous.** In spite of the importance given to it by European writers, it is probably nothing more than an **aberration.** The panel is about one foot square

with a semi-circular top edge. It shows Orpheus seated on a rock in the shade of an overhanging tree and holding a bow in his right hand and an instrument similar to but apparently not a violin (*Dixon-IJ*-II, ref. 52) in the playing position in his left. Several animals are seated round him. The **workmanship** of the panel is somewhat crude and scarcely to be compared with any other examples of *pietra-dura* inlay or mosaic in Delhi or Agra. It is positioned at the centre of the very top of the wall where whoever installed it must have known that it was least likely to be noticed." "The representation of Orpheus on the panel from early in the 19th century was said to have taken from one by Raphael. Fergusson called it 'a bad copy from Raphael's picture of Orpheus charming the beasts' which was in turn a copy of a picture in the catacombs (*Dixon-IJ*-II, ref. 53). However a perusal of the catalogues of Raphael's works (*Dixon-IJ*-II, ref. 54) reveals no representation of Orpheus. The nearest approach to the figure as depicted on the Delhi panel is that of Apollo in Raphael's Parnassus in the Stanza della Segnatura in the Vatican, but the posture, the clothing and the setting are all very different in the two pictures. Meyer-Baer suggests (*Dixon-IJ*-II, ref. 55) that in painting the Parnassus the persons of Apollo and Orpheus had merged in Raphael's mind and he compares Raphael's Apollo with a somewhat earlier Orpheus by Benedetto Montagna. This latter is nearer in some respects to the Delhi Orpheus (*Dixon-IJ*-II, ref. 56), but can certainly not be taken as its model. Nor is it possible to refer Raphael's Apollo or Benedetto Montagna's Orpheus to any painting in the catacombs of Rome (*Dixon-IJ*-II, ref. 57)"......"Whatever the model for the Orpheus and whatever the data it was produced or the date or reason why it was installed in the Diwan-i-Am, about which there is some doubt, it seems that the panel itself is of little consequence in the argument about the origin of Mughal inlay. In fact the belief that Italians were instrumental in either introducing or developing or producing designs for *pietra-dura* inlay in Mughal India rests on only slender foundations. . . . . **The notion in any case would not have flourished without the British sense of the inherent superiority of European culture** over the incomprehensible ways of life, of belief and of artistic expression with which they were surrounded in their Indian possessions" (*Dixon-IJ*-II, pp. 67-68).

19. *Ibid.*, p. 65 : **By 1844**, the Orpheus panel was widely known and adduced as European influence on Mughal art.

20. E.B. Havell also maintained that the solitary instance at the *Diwan-i-Am* in the Delhi Fort must have been **imported** (cf. *A Handbook to Agra and the Taj*, Calcutta, 1912, pp. 75, 90, 141). Percy Brown also agreed that this plaque was **imported from Florence** and "as a choice work of art was incorporated by the Indian artisan in his ornamental scheme just as a piece of exotic brocade might be included in a patchwork quilt" (cf. *Brown*, 105). In his opinion, the foreign influence in medieval India "was confined almost entirely to the field of minor and applied arts, the effect on the architecture being of little consequence owing mainly to its inherent constitutional vigour" (cf. *ibid.*, 105).

21 Cf. Archaeological Survey of India, Annual Report (hereinafter abb. *ASI AR*) 1911-12, p. 16. '*Taṣwīr*' denotes figurative painting.

22. E.B. Havell, *Essays on Indian Art, Industry and Education* (Madras, n. d.) pp. 13-14.

23. J. H. Marshall, "Conservation", *ASI AR* 1902-03, pp. 26-27.

24. Dixon also similarly noted that the motifs of Mughal inlay developed in India and they "seem to owe more to the geometric tradition in Islamic architectural decoration than to the influence of the contemporary European style of depicting flowers and plants **on the printed page**" cf. *Dixon-IJ*-II, 64-65.

25. Cf. *ASI AR* 1902-03, pp. 26-27, quoted above.

26. *ASI AR* 1904-05, pp. 2-3.

27. Dixon elaborated and confirmed this phenomenon : "The only Italian who is definitely on record as having been employed on work in *pietre-dure* in India is a certain Signor Menegatti, described as **'mosaicista'** whose services were obtained from Florence by the Archaeological Survey of India in 1906 to restore the wall containing the Orpheus and many other panels behind the throne-dais in the Delhi *Diwan-i-'Am*. Many of the stones used in the restoration were specially acquired from Florence, and Menegatti completed his task in 1909. The former Viceroy, Lord Curzon, made a substantial donation towards the cost of the work" (*Dixon-IJ*-II, p. 58; *ASI AR* 1911-12, p. 21).

28. *Ibid.*

2

Evolution of Inlay Art
in Mughal Architecture

The Mughal inlay called *pachchīkārī* or *parchīnkārī* **developed in India indigenously,** as the following examples of the Mughal period (even if we set aside examples of the Sultanate period, AD 1206-1526) — being distinct landmarks of the evolutionary process — unequivocally testify.

Humayun founded his ***Dīn-Panāh*** citadel (Old Fort) at Delhi in AH 939 / AD 1533 and its walls, bastions, ramparts and gates were finished in 1534.[1] There is a beautiful stylized lotus design, composed of eight petals ('*ardal*') containing an eight-pointed star, **inlaid** with white marble on a red stone sunk panel, on either side of the archway, on the facade of its northern ***Talāqī-Darwāzah*.**[2] Spandrels of the *īwān*, finished in black slate stone, have rosettes of red stone in high relief.[3] It is here itself, as early as that, that the Mughal artisans' attempt to use stones of two different colours together, for architectural effect, is perceptible. The western ***Barā-Darwāzah*** is also built of dressed red sandstone with use of white marble and black slate for emphatic outlines.[4] A hexagonal motif appears above the archway, one on each spandrel. It is **inlaid** with red upon a white stone background[5] and, technically, this is also "**inlay**" which was executed here in 1533-34.

The *Sher-Mandal* in the same fort, built by Humāyūn contemporarily (1533-40), also has distinct specimens of "inlay." Hexagonal motifs have been used on the spandrels of its upper storey arches on all external sides. These are inlaid with white marble on a red stone background[6] (*Pl.* 7). There are thus (2×8=) 16 such inlaid motifs on this octagonal building. Every angle has a carved stone nook-shaft, flanked on either side, i.e., on the exterior, by a red stone square panel which bears a geometrical design **inlaid** with white marble with a border of black slate[7] (see *Pl.* 7). It is a 12-petalled flower with a 12-pointed star inside it. With the removal of a few white marble pieces of the design, their sockets are distinctly visible, testifying that these were "**laid in**," and, technically, it was an "inlay" work.

Most pronounced specimens of inlay, of this age, however, appear in the *Qal'ā-i-Kuhnā Masjid*, which was built by Humāyun in the same fort contemporarily.[8] Its central arch, on the facade, bears **inlay of coloured stones** in geometrical designs[9] (*Pls.* 5-6). White marble, yellow stone and black slate pieces have been inlaid in red stone; curiously, red stone pieces have also been used here for inlaying on white marble background. The intrados of the portal also bears inlaid and carved designs together (*Pl.* 8). It is, in fact, to this polychrome **inlay art** that this central portal owes such an unprecedented gorgeous and magnificent effect.

The *Tomb of Aṭagah Khān* at Delhi, datable to 1566-67, bears inlaid mosaics of white marble and black slate in red stone slabs on the exterior dados, along with mosaics of green and blue glazed tiles on white marble on spandrels of the arches[10] (*Pl.* 9). Though these geometrical designs are broad and bold, these have been

Pl. 5 Inlaid Designs on the Central Arch,
Qil'a-i-Kuhna Masjid (1533-40), Old Fort Delhi

Pl. 6 Inlaid Designs on the Central Arch,
Qil'a-i-Kuhna Masjid (1533-40), Old Fort Delhi

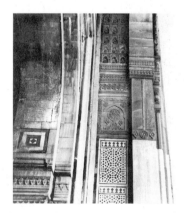

Pl. 7 Inlaid Designs, *Sher Mandal* (1533-40),
Old Fort Delhi

Pl. 8 Inlaid Designs on the Intrados,
Central Arch, *Qil'a-i-Kuhna Masjid*

Pl. 9 Inlaid Designs, *Tomb of Atagah Khan* (1566-67), Delhi

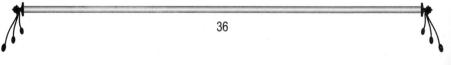

technically **"inlaid**." It is here that white marble has been used on this red stone building, on an unprecedentedly large scale **to highlight architectural lines, both horizontal and vertical,** of which phenomenon the *Tomb of Humāyun* (*c*. 1558-70), also at Delhi, is the most representative example. White and black marbles have been used on all edges, outlines of arches, friezes and also, intermittently, on oblong panels along with red and grey sandstones with which the tomb was finished[11] (*Pls*. 10-11). These have been skilfully **inlaid** in the background, and, technically, this is also an **"inlay"** art, which has not been used just for surface decoration, but for giving an exquisite **architectural complexion** to the building as a whole. Single colour monotony has, thus, been dispensed with, and this simple colour combination, in **natural stone tints**, has bestowed upon the *Tomb of Humāyun* an exceedingly tempered and pleasing effect — so needed in the tropical climate of Delhi.

Akbar started the reconstruction of Agra Fort in AH 972/AD 1565 and it was completed along with its palaces and other buildings, in 14 years' time.[12] The *Delhi-Gate* was its principal and formal gateway which was finished in 976/1568-69.[13] The *Hāthī-Pol* (the Elephant-Gate) is its inner gate where *naubat* (ceremonial music) was played. Two octagonal towers protect the entrance, one on its either side. Horizontal oblong panels above the second storey alcoves, just below the frieze and cornice, depict *gaja-vyāla*s (composite animals with elephant head) and ducks **inlaid with white marble on red stone background,** interspersed sparsely with black slate[14] (*Pl*. 12). There are 12½ panels on each side of the gate, alternatingly depicting a pair of *gaja-vyāla*s on the one[15] (*Pl*. 13) and a pair of ducks on the other[16] (*Pl*. 14), separated in the former case by a geometrical pattern, and in the latter by an Assyrian palmette.[17] While the *gaja-vyāla* and the accompanying seven elephants are of red stone, except its tusks and wings, and it is the background which has been **inlaid** with white marble —

Pl. 10 Tomb of Humayun (c. 1558-70), Delhi

Pl. 11   Inlaid Stone Work, *Tomb of Humayun*

Pl. 12   *Hathi-Pol*, Delhi Gate (1568-69) Agra Fort, with Inlaid Motifs

Pl. 13   Inlaid *Gaja-Vyalas*
(Composite animal with elephant-head),
Hathi-Pol, Agra Fort

Pl. 14   Inlaid Ducks, *Hathi-Pol,*
Agra Fort

technically **in the reverse order** — ducks have been inlaid with white marble on a red stone background. Borders in both cases have been similarly inlaid, and so is the intermediary geometrical design in the former case and the palmette in the latter. It is all **inlay art** executed here with total confidence and emphasis.[18]

The so-called *Jehāngīrī-Maḥal* which is the northern wing of Akbar's *Bengālī-Maḥal*, in the same fort,[19] was completed in 1569. Its western facade (*Pl.* 15) is composed of an arched portal in the centre (*Pl.* 16) and a series of ornamental arches on either side and an octagonal tower at the end of each wing. The frieze of the portal has geometrical designs **inlaid with white marble on a red stone background** (*Col. Pl.* VIII). Three hexagonal motifs have also been similarly inlaid inside it. Each ornamental arch of the wings is framed by a white marble fringe of lotus-buds, containing an ornamental arched niche of red stone, **in high relief, and it mounts it splendidly like a picture** (*Pl.* 17). These arches are repeated on the whole facade and on the towers, and also on the eastern facades of the palace (*Pl.* 18). It is here, more illustratively than at the *Tomb of Humāyun,* that the principle of juxtaposition of one stone with its unique characteristics against another stone with a different visual impact has been most logically, and effectively, presented. **This art is three-dimensional and is exclusively architectural** in which a beautiful effect has come by high relief and play of light-and-shadow and it was essentially **an indigenous development of the stone art of India** during the medieval period. It had nothing to do either with an Islamic art or a European art.

Examples of inlay may also be cited from *Jāmi' Masjid* of Fatehpur Sikri which was finished in 979/1571-72.[20] As in several other buildings of this township, greyish whitish, yellowish (so-called buff coloured) and pinkish stones have been used here along with red stone assertively and effectively on the gateways and facade of the *īwān*. Inlaid mosaics have also been used boldly on the eastern *Bādshāhī-Darwāzah* (*Pl.* 19) and the *Buland-Darwāzah*

Pl. 15 Western Façade of the (so-called) *Jehangiri Mahal* (1569), Agra Fort

Pl. 16 Inlaid Designs on the Portal, *Jehangiri-Mahal* Agra Fort

Pl. 17 White Marble Framing of Red Stone Arches,
Western Façade of the *Jehangiri Mahal* (1565-69), Agra Fort

Pl. 18 White Marble Framing of Red Stone Arches,
Eastern Façade of the *Jehangiri Mahal* (1565-69), Agra Fort

Pl. 19 Inlaid Designs, *Badshahi Darwazah, Jami' Masjid* (1564-72),
Fatehpur Sikri

Pl. 20 Inlay Work on the *Buland-Darwazah* (1601),
Jami' Masjid, Fatehpur Sikri

(*Pl.* 20) which replaced the original southern gate in 1601 to commemorate the conquest of the Deccan;[21] and on the *īwān*-portal of the mosque.[22] All these are geometrical designs, some belonging to the "star" group, which have been **inlaid with white marble and black slate pieces on a red stone background** (*Pl.* 21). Inlaid mosaics of both stones and glazed tiles[23] have also been used on the *Qiblah* wall, on the central and other *miḥrāb*s (*Pls.* 22-23, *Col. Pl.* IX). These are all geometrical designs of the star group. It is note-worthy that mosaic of glazed-tiles and stones in the inlay technique was rarely used in the interiors. It appears in the *Tomb of Atagah Khān* at Delhi around 1566-67 and in this mosque *c.* 1572, probably for the last time.

"**Inlay**" was a fully developed art by the time Jehāngīr acceded to the throne, in 1605. This fact is illustrated at the *Tomb of Akbar* (1605-12) Sikandara, Agra, where it is used, with total command, on the south (main) gate, on west and east (ornamental) gates, and on all the *īwān* portals of the main building.[24] The south gate (*Pls.* 24-25) has specimens of both mosaic of stones pieces of different colours "**laid over**" a stone slab which has no role to play in the make-up of the design, and mosaic of stone pieces of different colours "**laid in**" a stone slab which provides a background to the design. The latter is the "inlaid" mosaic, or "**inlay**" and it has been used judiciously and effectively together with the former along the whole mural surface, making up a simple geometrical design of white on red background or a bold naturalistic design of white, black and yellow stones also on a red background (*Pls.* 26 to 30, *Col. Pl.* X). White-and-red *chevron* design on nook-shafts attached to the wall which bears panels depicting white-and-red geometrical designs of the star group and white and black stylized arabesques in the spandrels of the ornamental arch — **are all so precisely inlaid as to look like a drawing on paper,** rather than a stone work. Some spandrels of the arches have stylized arabesques inlaid with black and yellow stones on white background asso-

Pl. 21   Inlaid Designs, *Jami, Masjid* (1564-72), Fatehpur Sikri

Pl. 22   Inlaid Designs on the *Mihrabs,*
Jami' Masjid (1564-72), Fatehpur Sikri

Pl. 23 Inlaid Designs on the *Mihrabs, Jami' Masjid* (1564-72),
Fatehpur Sikri

Pl. 24 Inlay and Mosaic on the Main (South) Gate,
Akbar's Tomb (1605-12), Sikandara Agra

Pl. 25   Inlay and Mosaic on the Main (South) Gate,
Akbar's Tomb (1605-12), Sikandara Agra

Pl. 26 Inlaid Designs on the Mural Surface,
Main (South) Gate, *Akbar's Tomb* (1605-12), Agra

Pl. 27   Inlaid Designs on the Mural Surface, Main Gate,
Akbar's Tomb (1605-12), Agra

Pl. 28   Inlaid Designs on the Mural Surface, Main Gate,
Akbar's Tomb (1605-12), Agra

Pl. 29   Inlaid Designs on the Mural Surface, Main Gate,
Akbar's Tomb (1605-12), Agra

Pl. 30   Inlaid Designs on the Mural Surface, Main Gate,
Akbar's Tomb (1605-12), Agra

ciated with another naturalistic floral design, within the arch, inlaid with white and black stones on red background, and the **combination of tints and tones is simply exquisite** (*Pls.* 31-32). Truly, this never happened anywhere else, and it also did not happen in India, the traditional home of stone art, before it, and the credit undoubtedly goes to the Mughals.

The main tomb has a magnificent *īwān*-portal in the middle of each side, contained in a broad frame, surmounted by a beautiful white marble *chhaparkhaṭ* (*Pl.* 33). This frame has been panelled in an order which corresponds with the *īwān* in giving emphasis on the vertical axis. Thus, there are seven panels on each side and seven on the top, but the two panels on the top corners being common to the sides, there are (6+7+6=) 19 panels in all. While the top panels are all square, there are only two square panels on each side (3rd and 5th from below). Two panels on each side are arch-shaped, with spandrels. All these 19 panels bear geometrical designs **inlaid** in white, black, yellow, green and red stones (*Col. Pl.* XI). Spandrels of its ornamental arches, as also those of the *īwān*, bear **inlaid** arabesques. The nook-shafts bear inlaid *chevron*. It is noteworthy that, originally, the whole facade, on each side, was similarly covered by inlaid designs, like the south gate. These exquisitely inlaid panels being prized curios for making table-tops as well as wall-hangings, were all plundered in the subsequent ages and the present red plaster is just an ad hoc restoration work done by the British.

Each of the western and eastern gates is occupying the middle of the respective enclosing wall *parkoṭā,* facing the respective causeway — with a large tank in its front, in accordance with the *chār-bāgh* plan, so that its *īwān* is in alignment with the central *īwān* of the main tomb. Each one is a monumental building which can stand independently anywhere else. The stupendous *īwān* on its facade is closed and it does not contain an archway as usual and it is just ornamental. It is not panelled; instead an **inlaid** geometrical

Pl. 31   Inlaid Stylized Arabesques on the Spandrels of Arch, Main Gate, *Akbar's Tomb* (1605-12), Agra

Pl. 32   Inlaid Stylized Arabesques on the Spandrels of Arch, Main Gate, *Akbar's Tomb* (1605-12), Agra

Pl. 33 Inlaid Panels on the *Iwan*-Portal, Main Tomb, *Akbar's Tomb* (1605-12), Agra

design is spread continuously on its sides and the top (*Pls.* 34-35). An oblong panel above the *īwān* bears an inlaid stylized arabesque design (*Pl.* 36). Its spandrels also bear inlaid arabesques, in two different colours, viz., green and white stone. *Ābrī* stone has also been used in some cases (*Pl.* 37). But, most frequently, it is a combination of red stone and white marble, either way. **A novel technique of inlay** has been adopted here, on spandrels of alcoves and oblong panels above them (*Pls.* 38-39). The arabesque design, in each case, has been carved in relief on a red stone slab, and the intermediary spaces of the design have been filled in, technically **inlaid,** by white marble pieces. Thus it appears that the design is spread on a white marble background, though it is made on a red stone slab. The effect of relief, instead of a plain, flat surface is simply exquisite. It is this beautiful way that the native artisan associated the Mughal inlay with his traditional relief-carving art. Inlaid designs have also been spread judiciously on the exterior of these gates (*Col. Pl.* XII).

Of singular importance, in this connection, are the three white marble **dados** which have survived in the second storey hall of the western gate. Each one is quite plain, except on the border which has a beautiful repetitive stylized floral design, inlaid by black marble and *ābrī* stones of chocolate-grey-yellowish colour (*Pl.* 40).[25] That these pieces were *laid in* to make up the design is testified by the blank sockets from which such pieces have been removed, and this is an illustrative example of the Mughal inlay art.

The 8-pointed star which is the key of this design and is repeated alternatively along the whole border deserves particular attention. It has first been inlaid with an 8-pointed *ābrī* piece, all internal points of which have small holes which were inlaid, most probably, by pearls or some other lustrous precious stone of yellow tint. They have ALL been carefully removed. Within this *ābrī* piece, another 8-pointed star of white marble is inlaid, which is further

Pl. 34   Inlay on the *Iwan*, Eastern Gate, *Akbar's Tomb* (1605-12), Agra

Pl. 35   Inlaid Designs, revealing sockets, Eastern Gate, *Akbar's Tomb*, Agra

Pl. 36 Inlaid Arabesques on the top and spandrels of the *Iwan*,
Western Gate, *Akbar's Tomb,* Agra

Pl. 37 Inlaid Designs, Western Gate, *Akbar's Tomb* (1605-12), Agra

Pl. 38 Inlaid White Marble on Red Stone Relief,
Eastern Gate, *Akbar's Tomb* (1605-12), Agra

Pl. 39   Inlaid White Marble on Red Stone Relief,
Eastern Gate, *Akbar's Tomb* (1605-12), Agra

Pl. 40   White Marble Dado, with Inlaid Border, Second Storey Hall,
Western Gate, *Akbar's Tomb,* Agra

inlaid by another 8-pointed star of black marble. Some semi-
precious stone of brilliant red or pink colour, e.g., coral or
cornelian, appears to have been finally inlaid into this black star —
to give this design a gorgeous appearance. This is a complicated
technique which the artisans could have mastered at the advanced
stages of the development of the art. Its execution here between
1605 and 1612 confirms that the art of inlay had reached a stage of
perfection even in the early years of Jehāngīr's reign — and it
makes no sense to attribute its introduction to Europeans. It is
noteworthy that all dado-panels in the second storey main halls of

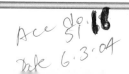

all gates had such inlaid dados, numbering more than a hundred, out of which only these three have survived.

It must be pointed out that Muhgal miniature paintings of Jehangir's reign were mounted with borders *hāshiyah*s which had **naturalistic floral designs,** frequently with birds and animals. Though the idea to mount a dado with a border of floral design was drawn from the contemporary art of Mughal painting, the border of the Mughal dado is invariably composed of a **stylized floral design** with no birds or animals.[26] The border style which makes a beginning here (1605-12), retains its spirit throughout the course of its development, as far as the Tāj Mahal (1631-48).

The *Tomb of I'timād-ud-Daulah* at Agra (1622-28) marks a step forward in the development of the inlay art. Unlike other buildings which had preceded it, it was externally finished, entirely, in **white marble** which needed only sparsely distributed ornamentation with carefully selected material. While tessellated type of mosaic was used on a large scale at the *Tomb of Akbar,* here the "**inlay**" type predominates and it is in this technique that most of the stone mosaic has been executed, though, of course, the tessellated type is not altogether absent and has been employed on some exterior panels. It is inlay, in the real sense, in which sliced rare and semi-precious stones are "**laid in**" specially hollowed sockets in the white marble slabs to make up a design. Undoubtedly, it owes its predominant use, from now onwards, to the adoption of white marble as the chief building material, instead of red sandstone. This grand sepulchre thus heralded the dawn of a new era when white marble completely replaced red stone, and mosaic gave way to the exquisite art of "**inlay**." This change in the style of decoration harmonized well with the change in the building material. All this was indigenous development.[27]

It eastern gateway (*Pl.* 41) which is of red stone has bold and

deep inlaid work with white marble pieces, in which scheme geometrical and stylized floral designs dominate. The *chevrons* on the nook-shafts and arabesques on the spandrels of the arches are similar to earlier examples at the **Tomb of Akbar.** A beautiful floral scroll has been used around the entrance, inside the *īwān.* There is no doubt that devoid of this inlay work, the gateway would loose much of its charm, and would become only one of the common-place buildings of medieval times scattered in and around Agra.

Almost the whole exterior of the main building (tomb) (*Pl.* 42) has inlaid work in geometrical, stylized floral and arabesque designs (*Pl.* 43), intermixed with *guldastā*s (plant compositions), wine-vases, cups and dishes, and cypress trees, on horizontal and vertical panels used together with perfect harmony (*Pls.* 44-45, *Col. Pl.* XIII). Spandrels of the arches have wonderful **arabesque** designs which appear to be floating on the triangular space (*Pl.* 46). The panels on the mural surface depict a wide variety of motifs and designs to avoid monotony of repetition. It is noteworthy that adequate plain and vacant surfaces have been associated with them for giving emphasis on the ornamental forms. Curiously, these designs have also been spread on towers (*Pls.* 47 & 48) and even pavements (*Pl.* 49). "**Exquisiteness**" is the watchword of this decoration.

It is "inlay" art executed with such marine products as *mūṅgā* (coral, deep red), *śaṅkha* (conch-shell, cream white) and *sīpa* (mother-of-pearl, white) and such rare stones as *ābrī* (colour : blackish golden); *ajūbā* (wonderstone, multi-colours on grey background); amethyst (purple or bluish violet); *aqīq* (agate, brown or blackish red); *bairūz* (aquamarine, light blue); *billaur* (crystal or quartz, transparent white); *dahanā* or *dānāfiraṅg* (malakite, light green pistachio); *dantlā* (yellowish white); *ḍūr* (brown); *firozā* (turquoise, sky blue); *hadīd* (greyish black); *jasper* (blackish green); *kaṅslā* (green-and-white); *kasauṭī* (deep black); *kaṭehlā* (violet); *khārā* (greenish black); *khattū* (a variety of agate, with multi-colours);

Pl. 41 Inlay Work on the Eastern (Main) Gate,
Tomb of I'timad-ud-Daulah (1622-28), Agra

Pl. 42   Tomb of *I'timad-ud-Daulah* (1622-28), Agra

Pl. 43   Inlay Work on the Exterior Mural Surface,
Tomb of I'timad-ud-Daulah (1622-28), Agra

Pl. 44   Inlaid Designs (*guldastas,* vases, cups and dishes),
Tomb of I'timad-ud-Daulah (1622-28), Agra

Pl. 45   Inlaid Designs (cypress, fruits, cup and dish),
Tomb of I'timad-ud-Daulah (1622-28), Agra

Pl. 46 Inlaid Arabesques on the Spandrels of Arch,
Tomb of I'timad-ud-Daulah (1622-28), Agra

Pl. 47   Inlaid Designs on Towers, *Tomb of I'timad-ud-Daulah*
(1622-28), Agra

Pl. 48   Inlaid Designs on Towers,
Tomb of I'timad-ud-Daulah (1622-28), Agra

Pl. 49   Inlaid Stylized Arabesque on the Pavement of the Upper Pavilion,
Tomb of I'timad-ud-Daulah (1622-28), Agra

lahsūniā (chrysolite or cat's eye, yellowish blue or red); *lājward* (lapis-lazuli, blue); *margaz* (light green); *maknātīs* (magnet-stone, lustrous greyish white); *mariam* (lustrous white); *namḍā* (blackish red); *shirgolā* (opal, different rainbow colours); *pai-zahar* (bamboo colour, yellowish light green); *pituniā* (bloodstone, red drops on blue background); *siyā* (deep black); *simāq* (red or yellow with yellow or pink spots); *sulaimānī* (onyx, white fibre on black background); *sunehlā* (cornelian, red); *tāmrā* (garnet, blackish red); *tilāī* (goldstone); *tilyar* (white spots on black); *yemenī* (deep red); *yashab* (jade, lustrous light green); and *zaharmorā* (whitish green), besides such common stones as *bādal, gaurī, gulābī, gwāliarī, lughiyā, rukham, mūsā* (or *chittoḍī, pīlū, reg* and *surkh*, of different tints and tones, and of such different geological rock-formations as sandstone, limestone, quartz, marble, schist, basalt and granite, which were obtained from Narmadā and Betwā valleys; regions of the Deccan plateau; Orissa, Rajasthan and Afghanistan; or quarried in the Braja region itself, at Karauli-Hindaun, Dholpur-Bari, Sar-Mathura, Tantpur, Bansi-Paharpur and Fatehpur-Sikri. All these have been used magnificently on white marble background. The whole building is covered by **stone-inlaid designs** in multiple colours, like the typical Iranian building which was also covered by **glazed-tiled designs,** in polychrome. But the difference between the two is too obvious to be missed. The former is a stone work, with a subdued and tempered colour complexion, and there is no glaze or lustre of the latter to offend the eye in this tropical climate. Precisely, it has a **natural colour effect,** like a flower-garden. Though built by an Iranian lady (Nūr Jehān) for her Iranian parents, its art has developed in India, in about a century's time, and it is essentially an **indigenous growth.**

It is the same inlay art which has been employed for orna-mentation of the white marble buildings of Shāh Jehān, in Agra Fort, Lahore Fort and Red Fort Delhi, with sophistication and refinement. The *Muthamman-Burj* **(Shāh-Burj)** of Agra Fort (1631-

40) bears inlaid designs on pillars, brackets, lintels (*Col. Pl.* XIV), dados, spandrels of arches (*Pl.* 50) and even in the water-basin sunk in its pavement (*Pl.* 51). While the dado-panels have naturalistic plant motifs, in relief carving, probably inspired by Ustād Manṣūr's compositions, with Chinese cloud forms '*Tchi*' which also came from Mughal painting — filling in the upper blank spaces, their borders have stylized floral scrolls inlaid by rare and semi-precious stones (*Pl.* 52). The dados of the *Dīwān-i-Khāṣ* (1635) (*Pl.* 53) in the same fort are more refined and sophisticated and mark the stage for the wonderful *ghaṭa-pallava* (vase-and-foliage) dados of the *Tāj Maḥal*; design of its inlaid border has been completely stylized, and it frames the exquisite plant compositions of the panel, in high relief, marvellously. An inlaid design also frames the *ghaṭa-pallava* composition, in relief carving, on the bases of its pillars (*Pl.* 54) with a wonderful aesthetic effect, similarly. It is this masterly way that the art of stone-carving and the art of stone-inlaying have been used together for ornamentation, for acceleration of **architectural nuances**! Similar examples of inlay work are there in the *Shish-Maḥal* palace complex of Lahore Fort;[28] and in the *Shāh-Burj, Dīwān-i-Khāṣ, Raṅg-Maḥal* and other buildings in the Red Fort Delhi (1639-48). Floral designs have been tastefully inlaid, with rare and semi-precious stones on the dados and piers of the *Dīwān-i-Khāṣ*, for example. Inlay in the *Raṅg-Maḥal* has been presented most beautifully in the shallow marble basin (*Pl.* 55) sunk in the central bay occupying its entire span of 20 ft side. The basin has been excellently designed and, with water bubbling softly from the slender fountain over the inlaid plants and flowers, it created a **magical charisma;** for, when it rippled from the edges of the inlaid petals, it produced effects of optical illusion and the petals appeared to rise and fall!

And the most refined and exquisite examples of inlay-art are, of course, there in the *Tāj Maḥal* (1631-48) on dados, spandrels of arches, tombstones, *jhajjharī* and other mural surface. All the four

Pl. 50   Inlay Art on the Dados, Spandrels and other
Mural Surface, *Muthamman Burj* (*Shah Burj*) (1631-40), Agra Fort

Pl. 51 Inlaid Water-Basin, sunk in the Pavement,
Muthamman Burj (*Shah Burj*) (1631-40), Agra Fort

Pl. 52 Dado with Inlaid Border,
Muthamman Burj Shah Burj (1631-40), Agra Fort

Pl. 53   Dado with Inlaid Border, *Diwan-i-Khas* (1635), Agra Fort

Pl. 54 Inlaid Designs with *Ghata-Pallava,*
Bases of Pillars, *Diwan-i-Khas* (1635), Agra Fort

portals *īwān*s of the main mausoleum have series of dados *izarah* with naturalistic floral motif (i.e., plant with twigs, flowers and leaves, with natural twists and turns) **carved in bold relief** in the centre of the panel in single series, and stylized repetitive creeper pattern **inlaid in polychrome** on the border *hāshiyah*, flowing rhythmically on the flat surface of the panel, all this stone work being composed harmoniously on a white marble background (*Pl.* 56, *Col. Pl.* XV).The dados of the main octagonal cenotaph-hall are unique (*Pl.* 57). The plant motif *guldastā* with leaves, flowers and twigs has been composed with a water-vase *pūrṇa-kalaśa, kumbha* or *ghaṭa* imparting it a distinct individuality of its own on the panel, which is lacking in the portal dados of the Tāj, or earlier dados of

Agra Fort. It is, in fact, from a vase, in each case, that luxurious vegetation — slender twigs, twisting leaves and bold flowers — emits and overspreads, exactly like the *ghaṭa-pallava* (vase-and-foliage) of ancient Indian Architecture and there is no doubt that the latter was the source of the former' s art. It is a **novel** feature in Mughal Architecture. It must, however, be noted that the vase-and-foliage of the Tāj is only a formal design used here for its sheer aesthetic appeal, and here it has no metaphysical meaning *artha*, symbolic purpose *prayojana* or auspicious character *śubha, maṅgala* with which its ancient prototype *ghaṭa-pallava* was invested.

The constituents also differ. There is no lotus (*padma*) flower and no mango (*āmra*) or *aśoka* leaves of the ancient *ghaṭa-pallava* and the plants of these dados, beginning with the **Muthamman Burj** of Agra Fort, have been adopted from tulip, iris, velvet, narcissus, lily, jonquil, marguerite and other botanical studies which were being painted on Mughal miniatures[29] since Ustād Manṣūr Naqqāsh made this a class in itself during the reign of Jehangir.[30]

This plant composition (*guldastā*) combines majestically with the inlaid border which is a highly stylized pattern with set curves and twists which are repeated. Perfectly appropriate stones are used to present different tints of the design and, in fact, each inlaid motif has been separately done. This border provides a delicate framing to the vase-and-foliage (*guldastā*) compositions of the panel, and the co-relationship between the art of chiselling in the mass and volume of stone bringing about the beautiful play of the third-dimension, and **the art of inlaying on the flat surface of the border in line and colour,** is most pleasing. Nowhere else a naturalistic design has combined with stylized one more harmoniously.

These bas-reliefs are a unique contribution of India to the art of dado-ornamentation. It was painting, stucco or glazed-tiling, both in the *ḥauż* (centre) and *hāshiyah* (border) outside India, and the

Pl. 55 Inlaid Water-Basin, *Rang Mahal* (1639-48), Red Fort Delhi

Pl. 56 Portal Dado with Inlaid Border,
Taj Mahal (1631-48), Agra

Pl. 57 Dados of the Main Cenotaph-Hall, with
Ghata-Pallava and Inlaid Border, *Taj Mahal* (1631-48), Agra

overall emphasis was on the organization of the flat surface by line and colour only. Here, in contrast, the main design is carved in stone in bold relief and colour is only secondarily associated with this relief work, with the result that instead of a dazzling effect, it produces an extremely pleasant play of light-and-shadow in the subdued, almost mysterious light of the interior. The traditional stone artist of India has, once again, asserted himself on the bas-reliefs of the Tāj Maḥal which, as a work of art, remain unexcelled.

It must also be noted that, as was the case with Mughal painting in which more than one painter was engaged on a miniature, several artists collaborated on the making of a Mughal dado. Thus, there were:

1. an artist who **designed,** in actual size, the plant composition (*guldastā)* for the *hauż* (centre), and

2. a sculptor *gul-tarāsh, śilpīn* who actually **carved** it in stone;

3. an expert who **drew and painted** the design, in real colours, for the *hāshiyah* (border), and

4. an inlayer (*parchīnkār* or *pachchīkār*) who actually **inlaid** it in stone with rare and semi-precious stones; and

5. a master-artist who **planned** the dado, as a whole, supervised and coordinated the work of all these experts.

Several Persian manuscripts, related to the construction of the ***Tāj Maḥal***, have come down to us and they mention, unanimously, the names of such native artisans as *sang-tarāsh* (stone-cutters), *gul-tarāsh* (flower-carvers) and *pachchīkār*s or *parchīnkār*s (inlayers)[31] and **there is no European name.**

An exquisitely finished octagonal marble *jālī* screen a (*jhajjharī* or *muḥajjar*) encloses the cenotaphs. Highly stylized florals with similar borders have been inlaid on it. Inlay art has been combined here with fine *jālī*-work as gracefully as it is used with carving on the dados. It marks the most sophisticated phase of art when as many as 48 tiny pieces of multi-colour semi-precious stones were used in a single flower (*Pl.* 58) ! The inlay work of the cenotaph-hall of the *Tāj Maḥal* has rightly earned the title of *chef d'oeu-vre* of Indian art.

Marble cenotaphs have also been ornamented with polychrome **inlay** with floral and stylized designs (*Pl.* 59). Verses from the *Qurān* are inscribed in the hall around the arched niches (*nasheman*) and friezes; they are inlaid with black slate on white marble (*Pl.* 60). **Inlaid arabesques** on the spandrels of the arches in the interior, as well as the exterior (*Pls.* 61-62, *Col. Pl.* XVI), added magnificently to the overall aesthetic effect; resembling floral scrolls, they hang predominantly over the arch like the bunch of flowers over a rivulet flowing below.

There is no lithic monotony in the *Tāj Maḥal* and, everywhere, and on every architectural part, from the pavement to the dome, stone of one colour is **inlaid** into stone of another colour, e.g., black marble on white on the *mīnār*s (*Pl.* 63) and white marble on red sandstone on such subsidiary buildings as the *Masjid* and the *Jam' āt-Khānah,* in a wide variety of designs. The whole complex is technically finished by **inlay art,** in one form or the other, though in extremely subdued, almost imperceptible, tints and tones (*Pl.* 64).

All this shows that **Mughal inlay art developed indigenously** and it is a misnomer to call it by the Italian name '*Pietra dura.*'

This brief survey shows that, during the course of development of this particular form of ornamentation, right since 1535, down to the *Tāj Maḥal* (finished in 1648), the Mughals used the **"inlay"** art on:

Pl. 58 Jali Screen (*Jhajjhari*) with Inlaid Borders and Cresting,
Taj Mahal (1631-48), Agra

Pl. 59   Marble Cenotaphs with Inlaid Designs, *Taj Mahal* (1631-48), Agra

Pl. 60   Inlaid Quranic Verses, Cenotaph Hall, *Taj Mahal* (1631-48), Agra

Pl. 61   Inlaid Designs on Spandrels of Arches,
Turrets, Pinnacles and Friezes, *Taj Mahal* (1631-48), Agra

Pl. 62   Inlaid Arabesques on the Spandrels of the Arch,
Taj Mahal (1631-48), Agra

Pl. 63   Inlay Work on the *Minar, Taj Mahal* (1631-48), Agra

Pl. 64 Inlay Art on the *Taj Mahal* (1631-48) Agra,
in beautiful tints and tones

I. pavements (*farsh*) and water-basins (*ābshār*) sunk in pavements; and plinths;

II. dados (*izāra*)

III. other mural surface above the dados;

IV. pillars, brackets and lintels;

V. tombstones (*ta'wīz̤*);

VI. jalied curtain around the tombstones (*jhajjharī, maḥjar* or *muḥajjar*);

VII. spandrels of the arches; and

VIII. *mīnār*s, domes, *chhatrī*s and *bārāhdarī*s,

and other **architectural spaces.**[32] While **this art is architectural,** there is NO example of the architectural use of *pietra-dura* in any Mughal building of this period (1535-1648), except the solitary case of ***Orpheus plaques*** which were imported and placed there some time after Aurangzeb, as has been discussed above. These plaques do not occupy any position at any stage of the evolutionary process of the "**inlay**" art of the Imperial Mughals (AD 1526-1707). These plaques were imported readymade, like the English coach which was presented by Thomas Roe to Jehāngīr.[33] The solitary case of an imported English coach does not testify that Indian vehicles as *belgāḍī* (bullock-cart), *bahl*, *'araba* and *rath*, for example, were inspired by, and developed from, it. In either case, it was an exotic thing which was treated as **curio** only. **These plaques did not have any impact on the natural growth and development of the indige-**

References

1. *HMA*-I, 134-35.

2. *Ibid.*, 143 and Pls. XCVIII-XCIX.

3. *Ibid.*

4. *Ibid.*, 146 & Pl. CIV.

5. *Ibid.*

6. *Ibid.*, 151 & Pl. CXIII.

7. *Ibid.*, 151 & Pl. CXIV.

8. *HMA*-I 173; it may "be assigned to the period from 1533 to *c.* 1565, with an interval from 1535 to 1555 and, in all probability, it was completed along with the Tomb of Humayun."

9. *Ibid.*, 162 & Pls. CXXV to CXXVII.

10. *Ibid.*, 191 & Pls. CXXXIX-CXL.

11. *Ibid.*, 261, Pls. CLXI to CLXIX.

12. *HMA*-II, 109.

13. *Ibid.*, 111.

14. *Ibid.*, 113.

15. *Ibid.*, Pl. XXVII-A.

16. *Ibid.*, Pl. XXVIII.

17. For an interpretation whereof see *ibid.*, 113-17.

18. Hence Dixon is right when he noted : "The inlaying of one stone into a channel or recess gouged out of another was being practised **before the appearance of Europeans in Northern India;** it is hardly conceivable that Indian craftsmen in any material needed foreigners to teach them the advantages of a template; **lac or shellac is an indigenous product;** and the use of an obvious development once the practice of inlaying coloured stones into white marble was adopted," *Dixon-IJ*-II, p. 61.

19. *HMA*-II, 118-23.

20. *Ibid.*, 192.

21. *Ibid.*, 197-98.

22. *Ibid.*, 195.

23. *Ibid.*, 193.

24. *CDMA*, 61-62; for full details see *HMA*-III, 365-69, 380.

25. *CDMA*, 61-62.

26. The development of the Mughal dado-art has been discussed in "Dado Ornamentation in Mughal Architecture," *Medieval Indian History & Architecture* (New Delhi, 1995), 75-88.

27. Dixon aptly noted : "This sudden appearance of Mughal inlay in its almost mature perfection as a technique could be explained purely as native stone-workers' reaction to the new calls made upon them as a result of the decision of the court to introduce **marble as the facing stone**. . . ." "There could not have been a Florentine mosaicista to train native craftsmen in the art of inlaying . . . the new development was a local response to a new requirement to use new and more costly raw materials," *Dixon-IJ*-II, 62-63.

28. It has been studied in full details in the *HMA*-IV, Part 1, Chapter 4 under the sub-head :"Palaces of the Lahore Fort" (*c.* 1631; 1633-44).

29. For example, *Windsor*, Plates 5, 10, 37 and 39.

30. For example, the miniature entitled : "Western Asiatic Tulip", painted by Manṣūr, *c.* 1620, original in the Maulana Azad Library, Aligarh, exhibited in the India Exhibition, Metropolitan Museum of Art, New York (October 1985); miniature entitled "Tulip and Iris", Mughal, painted in early seventeeth century AD original with the Aga Khan Geneva, exhibited in India Exhibition at the Metropolitan Museum of Art, New York (October 1985); "Flower Study" from Dara Shukoh Album, Mughal *c.* 1635, original in the India Office Library and Records (Add. or. 3129) cf. The *Indian Heritage* (Court Life and Arts under Mughal Rule) Victoria and Albert Museum, London (Catalogue on the Eve of Festival of India, London) p. 67, Colour Pl. 6 Entry No. 62; and "Velvet" Mughal, mid-seventeeth century in the Chester Beatty Library, cf. *Ibid.*, p. 67, Colour Pl. 6 Entry No. 219 (Chinese Cloud Forms, Tchi, have also been depicted in this miniature). These compositions are exactly similar to the bas-reliefs of Shāh Jehān's white marble monuments.

31. For details whereof, see this author's *The Taj Mahal and Its Incarnation* (Jaipur, 1985) 19-43.

32. One wonders if these examples of Mughal *inlay* were known to Ebba Koch and, if so, did she classify them under *inlay* or *pietra-dura*, and whether she held that all this too was a Florentine art even under Humayun and Akbar ?

33. *HMA*-III, 85-86; *The Embassy of Sir Thomas Roe to India* (1615-19) (ed. W. Foster) (New Delhi, 1990) p. 90; *Jehangir-Namah* or *Tuzuk-i-Jahangiri* (Memoirs of Jehangir) (tr. by A. Rogers & H. Beveridge), 2 vols. in one (Delhi rep. 1968), I. 388. Jehangir was so fascinated by it that he got into it at night and had it drawn a little by his men; Roe referred to this coach (pp. 98-99) in his letter to the East India Company, dated 25 January 1616 and recorded that the King was greatly pleased by this gift.

❈ ❈ ❈

Col. Pl. I. Back Wall of the Throne-Balcony (*Jharokhā*), *Dīwān-i-'Ām*, Red Fort, Delhi.
(photo courtesy: Ebba Koch's *Śhah Jahan and Orpheus*)

Col. Pl. II. Central Plaque depicting Orpheus playing to animals,
Throne-Balcony (*Jharokhā*), *Dīwān-i-'Ām*, Red Fort Delhi.
(photo courtesy: Ebba Koch's *Śhah Jahan and Orpheus*)

Col. Pl. III. Plaque with bird, set on the side of a wooden cabinet,
Italy, 17th century
(photo courtesy: Ebba Koch's *Śhah Jahan and Orpheus*)

Col. Pl. IV. Vase with flowers, set on the central door of a wooden cabinet,
Italy, 17th century
(photo courtesy: Ebba Koch's *Śhah Jahan and Orpheus*)

Col. Pl. V. Wooden Cabinet with birds, flowers and flower vases in *pietra-dure*,
Italy, 17th century
(photo courtesy: Ebba Koch's *Śhah Jahan and Orpheus*)

Col. Pl. VI. Wooden Cabinet with a large plaque of Orpheus on the central door and small plaques with animals on the front of the drawers in *pietra-dura*, Italy, c. middle of the 17th century, Chirk Castle, Cloyd, Greet Britain

(photo courtesy: Ebba Koch's *Shah Jahan and Orpheus*)

Col. Pl. VII. Inlay Art on the Throne Pavilion, *Dīwān-i-'Ām* (1628-35), Agra Fort

Col. Pl. VIII. Inlaid Designs on the Entrance Portal of the
so-called *Jehāngīrī-Mahal* (1565-69), Agra Fort

Col. Pl. IX. Inlaid Designs on the *Qiblah* Wall of the
Jāmi' Masjid (1564-72), Fatehpur Sikri

Col. Pl. X. Inlaid Designs on the
Main (South) Gateway of Akbar's Tomb (1605-12), Sikandara Agra

Col. Pl. XI. Inlaid Designs on the *Īwān*-Portal of the
Main Building, Akbar's Tomb (1605-12) Agra

Col. Pl. XII. Inlaid Designs on the Exterior of the
Western Gate, Akbar's Tomb (1605-12), Agra

Col. Pl. XIII. Inlaid Designs on the Exterior of the Tomb of I'timād-ud Daulah (1622-28), Agra

Col. Pl. XIV. Inlaid Designs, *Muthamman Burj*
(*Shāh-Burj*) (1631-40), Agra Fort

Col. Pl. XV. Inlaid Dados, Tāj Maḥal (1631-48), Agra

Col. Pl. XVI. Inlaid Spandrels of Arch, Tāj Maḥal (1631-48), Agra

Appendix

Mughal Forms:
Exotic or Indigenous

Ebba Koch's is the most controversial of the recent studies of this subject,[1] and it is necessary to examine and review her theories in some details.

She is just misinterpreting Jehangir's unusual, almost childish, fascination for European *curios* as "**Mughals' systematic interest.**"[2] His was an innocent curiosity in European things[3] presented to him, of which there are innumerous references in the accounts of foreign travellers of his age. If there was any influence, on the course of the development of a fine art, it was confined to certain motifs in Painting which were used sparingly as exotic phenomenon, and were never absorbed in the main current. **Those idioms were not translated in stone**, as is unmistakably illustrated by the fact that Mughal dados, though inspired by borders (*hāshiyah*s)[4] of Mughal Painting, did not depict birds or beasts of the latter. If Jehangir had an equally unusual interest in the breeding of goats, as his own *Memoirs* testify,[5] it did not mean that his was "Mughal's systematic interest" in veterinary science, and a veterinary influence on Mughal Architecture!

Shāh Jehān did not have even that curiosity in Europeans (towards whom his antagonism is well known), or in their things and, in his age, it was a natural growth and development of the style in which an ornamental motif here, or a design there, could have been inspired by an exotic element, but it was not an *influence* in the sense of *adoptation, borrowing* or *imitation*; it was an **"inspiration"** pure and simple, which was accepted in its own indigenous form. As far as the main current of the evolution of Mughal Architecture is concerned, European motifs, idioms or forms did not play any role whatsoever.

She discusses the influence of European idioms on Mughal painting,[6] with the help of a few selected miniatures, most frequently. Even if it is conceded, for a moment, for argument's sake, how can this influence be automatically transferred to Mughal Architecture ? She cites example of the *jharokhā banglā*[7] of the **Dīwān-i-'Ām** of Red Fort Delhi, and uses the term *'baluster columns'* for its pillars. She compares them with her *fig.* 3 of a **painting** showing Durer Circle, Triumphal Car from the Triumph of Maximilian-I, 1526. It is wrong to call these *bangla* pillars *balusters* or *baluster-columns*. **It is not baluster,** which is an upright support of a railing and which does not take a superincumbent load. Here, these pillars are supporting a *bānglādār* triangular ceiling and a superstructure. It is, in fact a *pillaret*[8] (= *stambhikā*, a smaller and refined version of *pillar* or *stambha* with feminine tenderness), While *pillar* or *pillaret* is structural, *baluster* is primarily ornamental, but Koch does not distinguish between these two different architectural elements.

The only other example of such *baluster columns*, she cites, is the throne-balcony of the *Machchhī-Bhawan* in Agra Fort. It is not original. It was restored by Stratchy in eighteen-eighties, as the Restoration Plaque placed on its eastern wall testifies.[9] It must be borne in mind, in this connection, that the Mughals, from Babur to Shāh Jehān (1526-1658), did not use full **semi-circular arch structurally,** and the few examples are only ornamental. Curiously, she does not point out any European influence in the throne-balcony of the *Dīwān-i-'Ām* of Agra Fort, or of Lahore Fort, or in similar buildings at Ajmer and Bari[10] which also belong to the same style and the same age. She wants to establish an "**influence**" on such a creative, versatile and prolific architectural style as the Mughal Architecture by a single and solitary example ? A single example could be an exception; and **no generalization** can be made on the basis of a single example either in case of *Orpheus plaques* or *Durer baluster*. It is all her subjective interpretation. Art-History is a strict discipline and, one wonders, if subjectivity can be stretched to such an extent.

Koch does not cite any documentary evidence to establish connection between these pillarets and the *Durer balusters,* and the only evidence she has in support of this contention is their "**visual resemblance**." In fact, *resemblance*, rather than docu-mentary sources of history, is her only tool which she uses a little too freely to be credible. That "**resemblance**," or **similarity of appearance, without the interconnecting links in Time and Space,** is an altogether deceptive methodology of art-history, has already been discussed, with reference to her other writings, by this author.[11]

This pavilion is, in fact, a *banglā* and it has been called a *banglā* by contemporary Persian historians as Lahauri and Kambo.[12] The course of the development of the *bānglādār* feature, in Shahjehanian architecture, can be systematically traced from the **Khās-Maḥal** Agra Fort (1631-40) to the **Motī-Masjid** Red Fort Delhi (1658-59), with numerous illustrative examples of ceiling-formation and facade composition. The pillaret of this *banglā* was also a **natural and corresponding development** — with segmental circular (less than semi-circular) arches-and-*chhajjā*s, and **pre-dominance of curved lines so much so that there is practically no straight line along its elevation.** Hence, it was also, accordingly, moulded, refined and sophisticated. The conceptual inspiration came from the *ghaṭa-pallava* pillars of the traditional Indian Architecture of this region itself, through the native artisans employed by the Mughals, rather than from any *Durer* or other European models situated thousands of miles away. Such pillars were, therefore, called in native artisans' vocabulary, *ghaṭaka* (from *ghaṭa* or *kalaśa* = water-vase or pitcher), and *padmaka* (grown from *padma* = lotus) whenever shown with lotus petals.

It is important to note that Lāhaurī, Kambo or any other contemporary or later contemporary historian does not at all allude to participation of any European artist, or import of European models for doing this work, and Koch does not explain how the *Durer* painting, showing *balusters*, reached Shāh Jehān's court to enable his artisans to copy them in the pillarets of the *jharokhā banglā* of the *Dīwān-i-'Ām* Red Fort Delhi. A European borrowing is Koch's own surmise which is not sustainable, with overwhelming evidence to the contrary.

As it appears, perhaps, **she writes for an exclusive white clientele** only. She has used the term *baluster columns* for Kambo's *sutūn* (= pillar or pillaret) and *baldachin* for his *banglā*, for example, so that her white clientele could easily understand them. All these terms are wrong and misleading. The substantial difference between *baluster* and *pillaret* has already been shown above. *Baldachin* is a cloth canopy, or an ornamental structure resembling a canopy, spread over an important person or a sacred object as altar, something like Mughal *chandovā*. As shown above, *banglā* is different. It is an architecture and, for that matter, such a substantial architecture that Lāhaurī has used this term for the large side-pavilion of the **Khāṣ-Maḥal** of Agra Fort. *Baldachin* does not denote a *banglā*, the same way *kiosk* does not denote a Mughal *chhatrī, chhaparkhaṭ, chaukhaṇḍī* or *bārāhdarī*.

She is, in fact, trying to impose her pre-conceived notions, as much as her own views and feelings upon this study. On this tendency of the European authors, my Late friend Jack S. Dixon, an Englishman and a perfect gentleman, aptly commented:

> In fact, the belief that Italians were instrumental in either introducing or developing or producing designs for *pietra-dura* inlay in Mughal India rests on only slender founda-tions. . . . The notion, in any case, would not have flourished **without the British (read European) sense of inherent superiority of European culture.**[13]

There is absolutely no doubt that it is this superiority complex which determined her theories of European influence on Mughal architecture, rather than plain and simple historical data. That is why, her writings are all argumentative, based on one or two exceptional examples, with practically no data.

Architecture is a difficult discipline and **identification of its original fabric** is the key to its understanding. The study will lead into blind alleys if one interprets a later restoration, renovation or addition in terms of the original, as Ebba Koch does in the present case. She does not know that *Orpheus plaques* were not there during Shāh Jehān's or Aurangzeb's reign, and these imported pieces were placed there later : between the period from 1707 (death of Aurangzeb) and 1824 when Bishop Heber noticed them there **for the first time.** There is no earlier record. Her attempt to assign these plaques to the art of Shāh Jehān, or to the art of the Great Mughals, for that matter, and interpret them accordingly, is **anachronistic,** and fundamentally wrong and misleading.

It is not necessary here to examine the validity or reasonable-ness of her use of such terms as *prototypes* or *Solomonic symbolism*, in respect of the evolution of Mughal architecture. While she uses the former term too lightly to warrant any serious consideration, she uses the latter one without any relevance to it. Fear and respect were pillars of medieval polity and a large number of epithets (*birudas*) were used by the Mughal king for exhibition and assertion of his power and prestige, and glory and grandeur of his rule; these epithets have hardly anything to do with the development of such a fine art as Architecture. Much of what she has written and illustrated in her book : *Shah Jahan and Orpheus* is wide off the mark, and is not relevant in the context of the study of Mughal *inlay* art.

It must also be pointed out that not only her interpretations, her identifications are also wrong, by and large. For example, she identifies the throne depicted in her pl. 47 as the *Peacock Throne (Takht-i-Ṭāus).* This in NOT the *Peacock Throne* of which we have an eye-witness description in Lahauri's *Bādshāh-Nāmah.*[14] He recorded that 20,000 *tolās* of jewels and 1,00,000 *tolās* of gold were used in its construction. Its roof (canopy or *chhatra*) was supported by **twelve (12)** emerald-coloured **pillars.** On the top of the canopy, **on each side, there were two**

peacocks, made of jewels, and between each pair there was a tree set with rubies, diamonds, emeralds and pearls. **Eleven (11) jewelled slabs** (*takiās*) were used as balustrade between the 12 pillars. Qudsi's panegyric, which Lahauri quoted in full, was written in green enamel (*mīnā*) inside.[15]   The throne depicted in her pl. 47 has four pillars only, instead of Lahauri's twelve; crude figures of only two peacocks on the finial, not two on each side, and no tree between them; and only five slabs (*takiās*) as balustrade instead of Lahauri's eleven, and this cannot be the **Peacock Throne.** Whether she has raised this ordinary and commonplace *aurang* to the grand status of *Takht-i-Ṭāus* deli-berately or innocently, is not known.

References

1.   *Koch, op. cit.*

2.   She uses this fearful phrase in the opening paragraph of the Introduction of her book on "Orpheus" itself (*Koch,* p. 7) which shows that she had already assumed that the Mughals' systematic interest in European art was the moving force of their art, and she began this study with this "conclusion" in mind.

3.   For his personality, see *HMA*-III, 69-140.

4.   For details whereof, see *ibid.*, 125-26.

5.   Cf. *ibid.*, 82-83.

6.   For example *Koch,* pp. 8-9 and figs. 3, 4 with pls. 1, 2, 4, 5, 9, 14 as she lists.

7.   Koch's understanding of *'banglā'* as a pavilion "vaulted with the curved roof" (*Koch,* p. 38, note 15) is wrong. There is no vault or arch. It is *'ladāo'* and the ceiling is *bānglādār*. It has been used in several other buildings of Red Fort, for which see *HMA*-IV Part 1.

8.   *'Pillaret'* from *'pillar,'* as *'minaret'* from *'minār'*.

9.   For full details, see *HMA*-IV, Part 1, Chapter 4 (a) (4): The Machchhī-Bhawan Complex.

10.   For which see *HMA*-IV, Part 1, Chapters 4 and 5.

11.   " 'Resemblance' as a Source of Mughal Architecture" in *Medieval Indian History & Architecture* (New Delhi, 1995) 123-26.

12.   For example, see her own reference to Kambo, *Koch,* pp. 12-13.

13.   *Dixon-IJ*-II, pp. 67-68.

14.   *BNL*, I. II. 78-81.

15.   For full details of the *Peacock Throne*, see *HMA*-IV, Part 1, Chapter 2 (c) (2) V.

Index

Afghanistan, 75
Agra, 23-24, 27
Agra Fort, 24, 37, 75, 82, 110
Ajmer, 111
Akbar, 20, 37, 42, 47
Aleppo, 24
Atagah Khān, 33, 47
Aurangzeb, 23, 25-26, 28, 113
Austin (Augustine) of Bordeaux, 19

Babur, 111
Bādshāhī-Darwāzah, 42
Bādshāh-Nāmah, 114
Bansi-Paharpur, 75
Barā-Darwāzah, 32
Bari, 75, 111
Bengālī-Maḥal, 42
Bernier, Francis, 23
Betwa, 75
Buland-Darwāzah, 42

Chaul, 19
Cole, Major H.H, 27

Delhi, 19, 23-24, 26, 28, 32-33, 37, 47, 110-11
Delhi-Gate (Agra Fort), 37
Dholpur, 75
Dīn-panāh (Old Fort Delhi), 19, 32
Dīwān-i-'Ām, Agra Fort, 21, 111
Dīwān-i-'Ām, Red Fort Delhi, 13, 19, 21, 23-24, 110, 112
Dīwān-i-Khāṣ, Agra Fort, 76
Dīwān-i-Khāṣ, Red Fort Delhi, 76
Dixon, Jack S., 28-31, 113
Durer Baluster, 111
Durer Circle, 110, 112

East India Co, 25

Fatehpur Sikri, 42, 75
Fergusson, James, 24
Florence, 28

Hāthī-Pol (Agra Fort), 37
Havell, E.B., 26
Heber, Bishop, 24, 113
Hindaun, 75

Humāyūn, 17, 19- 20, 32-33, 37, 42

India, 57, 75, 82
Italy, 28

Jehāngīr, 20, 47, 82, 94, 109
Jehāngīrī-Maḥal, 42
Jeronimo Veroneo, 19
Jones (Captain Sir John), 24, 27

Kambo, 25, 111-12
Karauli, 75
Khāṣ-Maḥal, Agra Fort, 26, 111-12
Koch, Ebba, 109-113

Lahore Fort, 75, 111
Lāhaurī, 23, 111-12, 114
Lando Bartoli, 21

Machchhī-Bhawan, 110
Mandu, 27
Manṣūr (Naqqāsh), Ustād, 76, 82
Marshall (John), 21, 26-27
Maximilian-I, 110
Menegatti, S., 28
Moti-Masjid Red Fort Delhi, 111
Muthamman-Burj, 75, 82

Narmada, 75
Nūr Jehān, 75

Orissa, 75

Orpheus, 17, 25-26
Orpheus Plaques, 13, 17-21, 23-24, 26, 28, 94, 111, 113

Peacock Throne (*Takht-i-Ṭāus*), 114

Qal'a-i-Kuhnā Masjid, 33
Qudsī, 114

Rajasthan, 75
Rang-Maḥal Red Fort, 76
Red Fort Delhi, 13, 19, 21, 23-25, 75, 110-11
Roe, Thomas, 94

Sar-Mathura, 75
Shāh-Burj (Agra Fort), 75
Shāh-Burj (Red Fort), 76
Shah Jehan, 17, 19-20, 23-24, 26, 75, 110-13
Shāhjehānābād, 19
Sher-Mandal, 33
Shīsh-Maḥal, Agra Fort, 24
Shīsh-Maḥal, Lahore Fort, 76
Sikandara, 47
Stratchy, 110

Talāqī-Darwāzah, 32
Taj Mahal, 13, 19, 66, 76, 81-82, 85-86
Tantpur, 75
Tomb of Akbar, 46, 66-67
Tomb of I'timād-ud-Daulah, 66

Acc No. 5116
Date 6.3.04

The book studies 'INLAY' art as it developed in Mughal Architecture indigenously, from Humāyūn to Shāh Jehān (*c.* 1535 to 1658 AD), landmark examples of which have been illustrated. Mughal inlay is architectural, and it is a misnomer to brand it: '*pietra-dura*' which was a florentine picture-art used on wooden furniture.

'Orpheus Plaques' which led the colonial historians to trace origin of Mughal inlay to Florence, were imported ready-made and there is no other example of Florentine *pietra-dura*. Inlay is the most distinctive characteristic of Mughal Architecture and study of its growth and development, to the elegance of the Taj dados, the *chef d'oeu-vre* of Indian art, is historically as enlightening, as interesting it is artistically.

Professor R. Nath (b. 1933), M.A., Ph.D., D. Litt, taught History at Agra College and University of Rajasthan Jaipur, from where he retired as Professor & Head of Department of History & Indian Culture. For almost half a century, he has been studying Indian historical architecture, chiefly Mughal Architecture, on which subject he has authored 55 books, 15 monographs and 179 research-papers, including the multi-volume series: *History of Mughal Architecture*. With his knowledge of Sanskrit and Persian, he writes authoritatively. His is, essentially, a study of the *Land*, the *People* and the *Culture*.

2004, 116 p.; 64 b/w photos; 16 coloured photos; 22 cm.

ISBN 81-246-0261-1 (PB)   **Rs. 280**

 D.K. Printworld (P) Ltd.

'*Sri Kunj*', F-52 Bali Nagar, NEW DELHI - 110 015
Phs.: (011) 2545 3975, 2546 6019;   Fax: (011) 2546 5926
E-mail: dkprintworld@vsnl.net   Web: www.dkprintworld.com